Marcel Proust: A Very Short Introduction

VERY SHORT INTRODUCTIONS are for anyone wanting a stimulating and accessible way into a new subject. They are written by experts, and have been translated into more than 45 different languages.

The series began in 1995, and now covers a wide variety of topics in every discipline. The VSI library currently contains over 750 volumes—a Very Short Introduction to everything from Psychology and Philosophy of Science to American History and Relativity—and continues to grow in every subject area.

Very Short Introductions available now:

ABOLITIONISM Richard S. Newman
THE ABRAHAMIC RELIGIONS
    Charles L. Cohen
ACCOUNTING Christopher Nobes
ADDICTION Keith Humphreys
ADOLESCENCE Peter K. Smith
THEODOR W. ADORNO
    Andrew Bowie
ADVERTISING Winston Fletcher
AERIAL WARFARE Frank Ledwidge
AESTHETICS Bence Nanay
AFRICAN AMERICAN HISTORY
    Jonathan Scott Holloway
AFRICAN AMERICAN RELIGION
    Eddie S. Glaude Jr.
AFRICAN HISTORY John Parker and
    Richard Rathbone
AFRICAN POLITICS Ian Taylor
AFRICAN RELIGIONS
    Jacob K. Olupona
AGEING Nancy A. Pachana
AGNOSTICISM Robin Le Poidevin
AGRICULTURE Paul Brassley and
    Richard Soffe
ALEXANDER THE GREAT
    Hugh Bowden
ALGEBRA Peter M. Higgins
AMERICAN BUSINESS HISTORY
    Walter A. Friedman
AMERICAN CULTURAL HISTORY
    Eric Avila
AMERICAN FOREIGN RELATIONS
    Andrew Preston
AMERICAN HISTORY Paul S. Boyer

AMERICAN IMMIGRATION
    David A. Gerber
AMERICAN INTELLECTUAL
    HISTORY
    Jennifer Ratner-Rosenhagen
THE AMERICAN JUDICIAL SYSTEM
    Charles L. Zelden
AMERICAN LEGAL HISTORY
    G. Edward White
AMERICAN MILITARY HISTORY
    Joseph T. Glatthaar
AMERICAN NAVAL HISTORY
    Craig L. Symonds
AMERICAN POETRY David Caplan
AMERICAN POLITICAL HISTORY
    Donald Critchlow
AMERICAN POLITICAL PARTIES
    AND ELECTIONS L. Sandy Maisel
AMERICAN POLITICS
    Richard M. Valelly
THE AMERICAN PRESIDENCY
    Charles O. Jones
THE AMERICAN REVOLUTION
    Robert J. Allison
AMERICAN SLAVERY
    Heather Andrea Williams
THE AMERICAN SOUTH
    Charles Reagan Wilson
THE AMERICAN WEST
    Stephen Aron
AMERICAN WOMEN'S HISTORY
    Susan Ware
AMPHIBIANS T. S. Kemp
ANAESTHESIA Aidan O'Donnell

ANALYTIC PHILOSOPHY
  Michael Beaney
ANARCHISM Alex Prichard
ANCIENT ASSYRIA Karen Radner
ANCIENT EGYPT Ian Shaw
ANCIENT EGYPTIAN ART AND
  ARCHITECTURE Christina Riggs
ANCIENT GREECE Paul Cartledge
ANCIENT GREEK AND
  ROMAN SCIENCE Liba Taub
THE ANCIENT NEAR EAST
  Amanda H. Podany
ANCIENT PHILOSOPHY Julia Annas
ANCIENT WARFARE
  Harry Sidebottom
ANGELS David Albert Jones
ANGLICANISM Mark Chapman
THE ANGLO-SAXON AGE John Blair
ANIMAL BEHAVIOUR
  Tristram D. Wyatt
THE ANIMAL KINGDOM
  Peter Holland
ANIMAL RIGHTS David DeGrazia
ANSELM Thomas Williams
THE ANTARCTIC Klaus Dodds
ANTHROPOCENE Erle C. Ellis
ANTISEMITISM Steven Beller
ANXIETY Daniel Freeman and
  Jason Freeman
THE APOCRYPHAL GOSPELS
  Paul Foster
APPLIED MATHEMATICS
  Alain Goriely
THOMAS AQUINAS Fergus Kerr
ARBITRATION Thomas Schultz and
  Thomas Grant
ARCHAEOLOGY Paul Bahn
ARCHITECTURE Andrew Ballantyne
THE ARCTIC Klaus Dodds and
  Jamie Woodward
HANNAH ARENDT Dana Villa
ARISTOCRACY William Doyle
ARISTOTLE Jonathan Barnes
ART HISTORY Dana Arnold
ART THEORY Cynthia Freeland
ARTIFICIAL INTELLIGENCE
  Margaret A. Boden
ASIAN AMERICAN HISTORY
  Madeline Y. Hsu
ASTROBIOLOGY David C. Catling

ASTROPHYSICS James Binney
ATHEISM Julian Baggini
THE ATMOSPHERE Paul I. Palmer
AUGUSTINE Henry Chadwick
JANE AUSTEN Tom Keymer
AUSTRALIA Kenneth Morgan
AUTHORITARIANISM James Loxton
AUTISM Uta Frith
AUTOBIOGRAPHY Laura Marcus
THE AVANT GARDE David Cottington
THE AZTECS Davíd Carrasco
BABYLONIA Trevor Bryce
BACTERIA Sebastian G. B. Amyes
BANKING John Goddard and
  John O. S. Wilson
BARTHES Jonathan Culler
THE BEATS David Sterritt
BEAUTY Roger Scruton
LUDWIG VAN BEETHOVEN
  Mark Evan Bonds
BEHAVIOURAL ECONOMICS
  Michelle Baddeley
BESTSELLERS John Sutherland
THE BIBLE John Riches
BIBLICAL ARCHAEOLOGY
  Eric H. Cline
BIG DATA Dawn E. Holmes
BIOCHEMISTRY Mark Lorch
BIODIVERSITY CONSERVATION
  David Macdonald
BIOGEOGRAPHY Mark V. Lomolino
BIOGRAPHY Hermione Lee
BIOMETRICS Michael Fairhurst
ELIZABETH BISHOP
  Jonathan F. S. Post
BLACK HOLES Katherine Blundell
BLASPHEMY Yvonne Sherwood
BLOOD Chris Cooper
THE BLUES Elijah Wald
THE BODY Chris Shilling
THE BOHEMIANS David Weir
NIELS BOHR J. L. Heilbron
THE BOOK OF COMMON PRAYER
  Brian Cummings
THE BOOK OF MORMON
  Terryl Givens
BORDERS Alexander C. Diener and
  Joshua Hagen
THE BRAIN Michael O'Shea
BRANDING Robert Jones

THE BRICS Andrew F. Cooper
BRITISH ARCHITECTURE
    Dana Arnold
BRITISH CINEMA Charles Barr
THE BRITISH CONSTITUTION
    Martin Loughlin
THE BRITISH EMPIRE Ashley Jackson
BRITISH POLITICS Tony Wright
BUDDHA Michael Carrithers
BUDDHISM Damien Keown
BUDDHIST ETHICS Damien Keown
BYZANTIUM Peter Sarris
CALVINISM Jon Balserak
ALBERT CAMUS Oliver Gloag
CANADA Donald Wright
CANCER Nicholas James
CAPITALISM James Fulcher
CATHOLICISM Gerald O'Collins
THE CATHOLIC REFORMATION
    James E. Kelly
CAUSATION Stephen Mumford and
    Rani Lill Anjum
THE CELL Terence Allen and
    Graham Cowling
THE CELTS Barry Cunliffe
CHAOS Leonard Smith
GEOFFREY CHAUCER David Wallace
CHEMISTRY Peter Atkins
CHILD PSYCHOLOGY Usha Goswami
CHILDREN'S LITERATURE
    Kimberley Reynolds
CHINESE LITERATURE Sabina Knight
CHOICE THEORY Michael Allingham
CHRISTIAN ART Beth Williamson
CHRISTIAN ETHICS D. Stephen Long
CHRISTIANITY Linda Woodhead
CIRCADIAN RHYTHMS
    Russell Foster and Leon Kreitzman
CITIZENSHIP Richard Bellamy
CITY PLANNING Carl Abbott
CIVIL ENGINEERING
    David Muir Wood
THE CIVIL RIGHTS MOVEMENT
    Thomas C. Holt
CIVIL WARS Monica Duffy Toft
CLASSICAL LITERATURE William Allan
CLASSICAL MYTHOLOGY
    Helen Morales
CLASSICS Mary Beard and
    John Henderson
CLAUSEWITZ Michael Howard
CLIMATE Mark Maslin
CLIMATE CHANGE Mark Maslin
CLINICAL PSYCHOLOGY
    Susan Llewelyn and
    Katie Aafjes-van Doorn
COGNITIVE BEHAVIOURAL
    THERAPY Freda McManus
COGNITIVE NEUROSCIENCE
    Richard Passingham
THE COLD WAR Robert J. McMahon
COLONIAL AMERICA Alan Taylor
COLONIAL LATIN AMERICAN
    LITERATURE Rolena Adorno
COMBINATORICS Robin Wilson
COMEDY Matthew Bevis
COMMUNISM Leslie Holmes
COMPARATIVE LAW Sabrina Ragone
    and Guido Smorto
COMPARATIVE LITERATURE
    Ben Hutchinson
COMPETITION AND ANTITRUST
    LAW Ariel Ezrachi
COMPLEXITY John H. Holland
THE COMPUTER Darrel Ince
COMPUTER SCIENCE Subrata Dasgupta
CONCENTRATION CAMPS
    Dan Stone
CONDENSED MATTER PHYSICS
    Ross H. McKenzie
CONFUCIANISM Daniel K. Gardner
THE CONQUISTADORS
    Matthew Restall and
    Felipe Fernández-Armesto
CONSCIENCE Paul Strohm
CONSCIOUSNESS Susan Blackmore
CONTEMPORARY ART
    Julian Stallabrass
CONTEMPORARY FICTION
    Robert Eaglestone
CONTINENTAL PHILOSOPHY
    Simon Critchley
COPERNICUS Owen Gingerich
CORAL REEFS Charles Sheppard
CORPORATE SOCIAL
    RESPONSIBILITY Jeremy Moon
CORRUPTION Leslie Holmes
COSMOLOGY Peter Coles
COUNTRY MUSIC Richard Carlin
CREATIVITY Vlad Glăveanu

CRIME FICTION Richard Bradford
CRIMINAL JUSTICE Julian V. Roberts
CRIMINOLOGY Tim Newburn
CRITICAL THEORY
    Stephen Eric Bronner
THE CRUSADES Christopher Tyerman
CRYPTOGRAPHY Sean Murphy and
    Rachel Player
CRYSTALLOGRAPHY A. M. Glazer
THE CULTURAL REVOLUTION
    Richard Curt Kraus
DADA AND SURREALISM
    David Hopkins
DANTE Peter Hainsworth and
    David Robey
DARWIN Jonathan Howard
THE DEAD SEA SCROLLS
    Timothy H. Lim
DECADENCE David Weir
DECOLONIZATION Dane Kennedy
DEMENTIA Kathleen Taylor
DEMOCRACY Naomi Zack
DEMOGRAPHY Sarah Harper
DEPRESSION Jan Scott and
    Mary Jane Tacchi
DERRIDA Simon Glendinning
DESCARTES Tom Sorell
DESERTS Nick Middleton
DESIGN John Heskett
DEVELOPMENT Ian Goldin
DEVELOPMENTAL BIOLOGY
    Lewis Wolpert
THE DEVIL Darren Oldridge
DIASPORA Kevin Kenny
CHARLES DICKENS Jenny Hartley
DICTIONARIES Lynda Mugglestone
DINOSAURS David Norman
DIPLOMATIC HISTORY
    Joseph M. Siracusa
DOCUMENTARY FILM
    Patricia Aufderheide
DOSTOEVSKY Deborah Martinsen
DREAMING J. Allan Hobson
DRUGS Les Iversen
DRUIDS Barry Cunliffe
DYNASTY Jeroen Duindam
DYSLEXIA Margaret J. Snowling
EARLY MUSIC Thomas Forrest Kelly
THE EARTH Martin Redfern
EARTH SYSTEM SCIENCE Tim Lenton

ECOLOGY Jaboury Ghazoul
ECONOMICS Partha Dasgupta
EDUCATION Gary Thomas
EGYPTIAN MYTH Geraldine Pinch
EIGHTEENTH-CENTURY BRITAIN
    Paul Langford
ELECTIONS L. Sandy Maisel and
    Jennifer A. Yoder
THE ELEMENTS Philip Ball
EMOTION Dylan Evans
EMPIRE Stephen Howe
EMPLOYMENT LAW David Cabrelli
ENERGY SYSTEMS Nick Jenkins
ENGELS Terrell Carver
ENGINEERING David Blockley
THE ENGLISH LANGUAGE
    Simon Horobin
ENGLISH LITERATURE Jonathan Bate
THE ENLIGHTENMENT
    John Robertson
ENTREPRENEURSHIP Paul Westhead
    and Mike Wright
ENVIRONMENTAL ECONOMICS
    Stephen Smith
ENVIRONMENTAL ETHICS
    Robin Attfield
ENVIRONMENTAL LAW
    Elizabeth Fisher
ENVIRONMENTAL POLITICS
    Andrew Dobson
ENZYMES Paul Engel
THE EPIC Anthony Welch
EPICUREANISM Catherine Wilson
EPIDEMIOLOGY Rodolfo Saracci
ETHICS Simon Blackburn
ETHNOMUSICOLOGY Timothy Rice
THE ETRUSCANS Christopher Smith
EUGENICS Philippa Levine
THE EUROPEAN UNION
    Simon Usherwood and John Pinder
EUROPEAN UNION LAW
    Anthony Arnull
EVANGELICALISM
    John G. Stackhouse Jr.
EVIL Luke Russell
EVOLUTION Brian and
    Deborah Charlesworth
EXISTENTIALISM Thomas Flynn
EXPLORATION Stewart A. Weaver
EXTINCTION Paul B. Wignall

THE EYE Michael Land
FAIRY TALE Marina Warner
FAITH Roger Trigg
FAMILY LAW Jonathan Herring
MICHAEL FARADAY
    Frank A. J. L. James
FASCISM Kevin Passmore
FASHION Rebecca Arnold
FEDERALISM Mark J. Rozell and
    Clyde Wilcox
FEMINISM Margaret Walters
FEMINIST PHILOSOPHY
    Katharine Jenkins
FILM Michael Wood
FILM MUSIC Kathryn Kalinak
FILM NOIR James Naremore
FIRE Andrew C. Scott
THE FIRST WORLD WAR
    Michael Howard
FLUID MECHANICS Eric Lauga
FOLK MUSIC Mark Slobin
FOOD John Krebs
FORENSIC PSYCHOLOGY
    David Canter
FORENSIC SCIENCE Jim Fraser
FORESTS Jaboury Ghazoul
FOSSILS Keith Thomson
FOUCAULT Gary Gutting
THE FOUNDING FATHERS
    R. B. Bernstein
FRACTALS Kenneth Falconer
FREE SPEECH Nigel Warburton
FREE WILL Thomas Pink
FREEMASONRY Andreas Önnerfors
FRENCH CINEMA Dudley Andrew
FRENCH LITERATURE John D. Lyons
FRENCH PHILOSOPHY
    Stephen Gaukroger and Knox Peden
THE FRENCH REVOLUTION
    William Doyle
FREUD Anthony Storr
FUNDAMENTALISM Malise Ruthven
FUNGI Nicholas P. Money
THE FUTURE Jennifer M. Gidley
FUTURSM Ara Merjian
GALAXIES John Gribbin
GALILEO Stillman Drake
GAME THEORY Ken Binmore
GANDHI Bhikhu Parekh
GARDEN HISTORY Gordon Campbell

GENDER HISTORY Antoinette Burton
GENES Jonathan Slack
GENIUS Andrew Robinson
GENOMICS John Archibald
GEOGRAPHY John Matthews and
    David Herbert
GEOLOGY Jan Zalasiewicz
GEOMETRY Maciej Dunajski
GEOPHYSICAL AND CLIMATE
    HAZARDS Bill McGuire
GEOPHYSICS William Lowrie
GEOPOLITICS Klaus Dodds
GERMAN LITERATURE
    Nicholas Boyle
GERMAN PHILOSOPHY
    Andrew Bowie
THE GHETTO Bryan Cheyette
GLACIATION David J. A. Evans
GLOBAL ECONOMIC HISTORY
    Robert C. Allen
GLOBAL ISLAM Nile Green
GLOBALIZATION Manfred B. Steger
GOD John Bowker
GÖDEL'S THEOREM A. W. Moore
GOETHE Ritchie Robertson
THE GOTHIC Nick Groom
GOVERNANCE Mark Bevir
GRAVITY Timothy Clifton
THE GREAT DEPRESSION AND
    THE NEW DEAL Eric Rauchway
THE GULAG Alan Barenberg
HABEAS CORPUS Amanda L. Tyler
HABERMAS James Gordon Finlayson
THE HABSBURG EMPIRE
    Martyn Rady
HAPPINESS Daniel M. Haybron
THE HARLEM RENAISSANCE
    Cheryl A. Wall
THE HEBREW BIBLE AS LITERATURE
    Tod Linafelt
HEGEL Peter Singer
HEIDEGGER Michael Inwood
THE HELLENISTIC AGE
    Peter Thonemann
HEREDITY John Waller
HERMENEUTICS Jens Zimmermann
HERODOTUS Jennifer T. Roberts
HIEROGLYPHS Penelope Wilson
HINDUISM Kim Knott
HISTORY John H. Arnold

THE HISTORY OF ASTRONOMY
  Michael Hoskin
THE HISTORY OF CHEMISTRY
  William H. Brock
THE HISTORY OF CHILDHOOD
  James Marten
THE HISTORY OF CINEMA
  Geoffrey Nowell-Smith
THE HISTORY OF COMPUTING
  Doron Swade
THE HISTORY OF EMOTIONS
  Thomas Dixon
THE HISTORY OF LIFE
  Michael Benton
THE HISTORY OF MATHEMATICS
  Jacqueline Stedall
THE HISTORY OF MEDICINE
  William Bynum
THE HISTORY OF PHYSICS
  J. L. Heilbron
THE HISTORY OF POLITICAL
  THOUGHT Richard Whatmore
THE HISTORY OF TIME
  Leofranc Holford-Strevens
HIV AND AIDS Alan Whiteside
HOBBES Richard Tuck
HOLLYWOOD Peter Decherney
THE HOLY ROMAN EMPIRE
  Joachim Whaley
HOME Michael Allen Fox
HOMER Barbara Graziosi
HORACE Llewelyn Morgan
HORMONES Martin Luck
HORROR Darryl Jones
HUMAN ANATOMY
  Leslie Klenerman
HUMAN EVOLUTION Bernard Wood
HUMAN PHYSIOLOGY
  Jamie A. Davies
HUMAN RESOURCE MANAGEMENT
  Adrian Wilkinson
HUMAN RIGHTS Andrew Clapham
HUMANISM Stephen Law
HUME James A. Harris
HUMOUR Noël Carroll
IBN SĪNĀ (AVICENNA)
  Peter Adamson
THE ICE AGE Jamie Woodward
IDENTITY Florian Coulmas
IDEOLOGY Michael Freeden

IMAGINATION
  Jennifer Gosetti-Ferencei
THE IMMUNE SYSTEM
  Paul Klenerman
INDIAN CINEMA Ashish Rajadhyaksha
INDIAN PHILOSOPHY Sue Hamilton
THE INDUSTRIAL REVOLUTION
  Robert C. Allen
INFECTIOUS DISEASE Marta L. Wayne
  and Benjamin M. Bolker
INFINITY Ian Stewart
INFORMATION Luciano Floridi
INNOVATION Mark Dodgson and
  David Gann
INTELLECTUAL PROPERTY
  Siva Vaidhyanathan
INTELLIGENCE Ian J. Deary
INTERNATIONAL LAW
  Vaughan Lowe
INTERNATIONAL MIGRATION
  Khalid Koser
INTERNATIONAL RELATIONS
  Christian Reus-Smit
INTERNATIONAL SECURITY
  Christopher S. Browning
INSECTS Simon Leather
INVASIVE SPECIES Julie Lockwood and
  Dustin Welbourne
IRAN Ali M. Ansari
ISLAM Malise Ruthven
ISLAMIC HISTORY Adam Silverstein
ISLAMIC LAW Mashood A. Baderin
ISOTOPES Rob Ellam
ITALIAN LITERATURE
  Peter Hainsworth and David Robey
HENRY JAMES Susan L. Mizruchi
JAPANESE LITERATURE Alan Tansman
JESUS Richard Bauckham
JEWISH HISTORY David N. Myers
JEWISH LITERATURE Ilan Stavans
JOURNALISM Ian Hargreaves
JAMES JOYCE Colin MacCabe
JUDAISM Norman Solomon
JUNG Anthony Stevens
THE JURY Renée Lettow Lerner
KABBALAH Joseph Dan
KAFKA Ritchie Robertson
KANT Roger Scruton
KEYNES Robert Skidelsky
KIERKEGAARD Patrick Gardiner

KNOWLEDGE Jennifer Nagel
THE KORAN Michael Cook
KOREA Michael J. Seth
LAKES Warwick F. Vincent
LANDSCAPE ARCHITECTURE
    Ian H. Thompson
LANDSCAPES AND
    GEOMORPHOLOGY
    Andrew Goudie and Heather Viles
LANGUAGES Stephen R. Anderson
LATE ANTIQUITY Gillian Clark
LAW Raymond Wacks
THE LAWS OF THERMODYNAMICS
    Peter Atkins
LEADERSHIP Keith Grint
LEARNING Mark Haselgrove
LEIBNIZ Maria Rosa Antognazza
C. S. LEWIS James Como
LIBERALISM Michael Freeden
LIGHT Ian Walmsley
LINCOLN Allen C. Guelzo
LINGUISTICS Peter Matthews
LITERARY THEORY Jonathan Culler
LOCKE John Dunn
LOGIC Graham Priest
LOVE Ronald de Sousa
MARTIN LUTHER Scott H. Hendrix
MACHIAVELLI Quentin Skinner
MADNESS Andrew Scull
MAGIC Owen Davies
MAGNA CARTA Nicholas Vincent
MAGNETISM Stephen Blundell
MALTHUS Donald Winch
MAMMALS T. S. Kemp
MANAGEMENT John Hendry
NELSON MANDELA Elleke Boehmer
MAO Delia Davin
MARINE BIOLOGY Philip V. Mladenov
MARKETING
    Kenneth Le Meunier-FitzHugh
THE MARQUIS DE SADE John Phillips
MARTYRDOM Jolyon Mitchell
MARX Peter Singer
MATERIALS Christopher Hall
MATHEMATICAL ANALYSIS
    Richard Earl
MATHEMATICAL FINANCE
    Mark H. A. Davis
MATHEMATICS Timothy Gowers
MATTER Geoff Cottrell

THE MAYA Matthew Restall and
    Amara Solari
MEANING Emma Borg and
    Sarah A. Fisher
THE MEANING OF LIFE
    Terry Eagleton
MEASUREMENT David Hand
MEDICAL ETHICS Michael Dunn and
    Tony Hope
MEDICAL LAW Charles Foster
MEDIEVAL BRITAIN John Gillingham
    and Ralph A. Griffiths
MEDIEVAL LITERATURE
    Elaine Treharne
MEDIEVAL PHILOSOPHY
    John Marenbon
MEMORY Jonathan K. Foster
METAPHYSICS Stephen Mumford
METHODISM William J. Abraham
THE MEXICAN REVOLUTION
    Alan Knight
MICROBIOLOGY Nicholas P. Money
MICROBIOMES Angela E. Douglas
MICROECONOMICS Avinash Dixit
MICROSCOPY Terence Allen
THE MIDDLE AGES Miri Rubin
MILITARY JUSTICE Eugene R. Fidell
MILITARY STRATEGY
    Antulio J. Echevarria II
JOHN STUART MILL Gregory Claeys
MINERALS David Vaughan
MIRACLES Yujin Nagasawa
MODERN ARCHITECTURE
    Adam Sharr
MODERN ART David Cottington
MODERN BRAZIL Anthony W. Pereira
MODERN CHINA Rana Mitter
MODERN DRAMA
    Kirsten E. Shepherd-Barr
MODERN FRANCE
    Vanessa R. Schwartz
MODERN INDIA Craig Jeffrey
MODERN IRELAND Senia Pašeta
MODERN ITALY Anna Cento Bull
MODERN JAPAN
    Christopher Goto-Jones
MODERN LATIN AMERICAN
    LITERATURE
    Roberto González Echevarría
MODERN WAR Richard English

MODERNISM Christopher Butler
MOLECULAR BIOLOGY Aysha Divan
    and Janice A. Royds
MOLECULES Philip Ball
MONASTICISM Stephen J. Davis
THE MONGOLS Morris Rossabi
MONTAIGNE William M. Hamlin
MOONS David A. Rothery
MORMONISM
    Richard Lyman Bushman
MOUNTAINS Martin F. Price
MUHAMMAD Jonathan A. C. Brown
MULTICULTURALISM Ali Rattansi
MULTILINGUALISM John C. Maher
MUSIC Nicholas Cook
MUSIC AND TECHNOLOGY
    Mark Katz
MYTH Robert A. Segal
NANOTECHNOLOGY Philip Moriarty
NAPOLEON David A. Bell
THE NAPOLEONIC WARS
    Mike Rapport
NATIONALISM Steven Grosby
NATIVE AMERICAN LITERATURE
    Sean Teuton
NAVIGATION Jim Bennett
NAZI GERMANY Jane Caplan
NEGOTIATION Carrie Menkel-Meadow
NEOLIBERALISM Manfred B. Steger
    and Ravi K. Roy
NETWORKS Guido Caldarelli and
    Michele Catanzaro
THE NEW TESTAMENT
    Luke Timothy Johnson
THE NEW TESTAMENT AS
    LITERATURE Kyle Keefer
NEWTON Robert Iliffe
NIETZSCHE Michael Tanner
NINETEENTH-CENTURY BRITAIN
    Christopher Harvie and
    H. C. G. Matthew
THE NORMAN CONQUEST
    George Garnett
NORTH AMERICAN INDIANS
    Theda Perdue and Michael D. Green
NORTHERN IRELAND
    Marc Mulholland
NOTHING Frank Close
NUCLEAR PHYSICS Frank Close
NUCLEAR POWER Maxwell Irvine

NUCLEAR WEAPONS
    Joseph M. Siracusa
NUMBER THEORY Robin Wilson
NUMBERS Peter M. Higgins
NUTRITION David A. Bender
OBJECTIVITY Stephen Gaukroger
OBSERVATIONAL ASTRONOMY
    Geoff Cottrell
OCEANS Dorrik Stow
THE OLD TESTAMENT
    Michael D. Coogan
THE ORCHESTRA D. Kern Holoman
ORGANIC CHEMISTRY
    Graham Patrick
ORGANIZATIONS Mary Jo Hatch
ORGANIZED CRIME
    Georgios A. Antonopoulos and
    Georgios Papanicolaou
ORTHODOX CHRISTIANITY
    A. Edward Siecienski
OVID Llewelyn Morgan
PAGANISM Owen Davies
PAKISTAN Pippa Virdee
THE PALESTINIAN-ISRAELI
    CONFLICT Martin Bunton
PANDEMICS Christian W. McMillen
PARTICLE PHYSICS Frank Close
PAUL E. P. Sanders
IVAN PAVLOV Daniel P. Todes
PEACE Oliver P. Richmond
PENTECOSTALISM William K. Kay
PERCEPTION Brian Rogers
THE PERIODIC TABLE Eric R. Scerri
PHILOSOPHICAL METHOD
    Timothy Williamson
PHILOSOPHY Edward Craig
PHILOSOPHY IN THE ISLAMIC
    WORLD Peter Adamson
PHILOSOPHY OF BIOLOGY
    Samir Okasha
PHILOSOPHY OF LAW
    Raymond Wacks
PHILOSOPHY OF MIND
    Barbara Gail Montero
PHILOSOPHY OF PHYSICS
    David Wallace
PHILOSOPHY OF SCIENCE
    Samir Okasha
PHILOSOPHY OF RELIGION
    Tim Bayne

PHOTOGRAPHY Steve Edwards
PHYSICAL CHEMISTRY Peter Atkins
PHYSICS Sidney Perkowitz
PILGRIMAGE Ian Reader
PLAGUE Paul Slack
PLANETARY SYSTEMS
    Raymond T. Pierrehumbert
PLANETS David A. Rothery
PLANTS Timothy Walker
PLATE TECTONICS Peter Molnar
SYLVIA PLATH Heather Clark
PLATO Julia Annas
POETRY Bernard O'Donoghue
POLITICAL PHILOSOPHY David Miller
POLITICS Kenneth Minogue
POLYGAMY Sarah M. S. Pearsall
POPULISM Cas Mudde and
    Cristóbal Rovira Kaltwasser
POSTCOLONIALISM
    Robert J. C. Young
POSTMODERNISM Christopher Butler
POSTSTRUCTURALISM
    Catherine Belsey
POVERTY Philip N. Jefferson
PREHISTORY Chris Gosden
PRESOCRATIC PHILOSOPHY
    Catherine Osborne
PRIVACY Raymond Wacks
PROBABILITY John Haigh
PROGRESSIVISM Walter Nugent
PROHIBITION W. J. Rorabaugh
PROJECTS Andrew Davies
PROTESTANTISM Mark A. Noll
MARCEL PROUST Joshua Landy
PSEUDOSCIENCE Michael D. Gordin
PSYCHIATRY Tom Burns
PSYCHOANALYSIS Daniel Pick
PSYCHOLINGUISTICS
    Ferenda Ferreria
PSYCHOLOGY Gillian Butler and
    Freda McManus
PSYCHOLOGY OF MUSIC
    Elizabeth Hellmuth Margulis
PSYCHOPATHY Essi Viding
PSYCHOTHERAPY Tom Burns and
    Eva Burns-Lundgren
PUBLIC ADMINISTRATION
    Stella Z. Theodoulou and Ravi K. Roy
PUBLIC HEALTH Virginia Berridge
PURITANISM Francis J. Bremer

THE QUAKERS Pink Dandelion
QUANTUM THEORY
    John Polkinghorne
RACISM Ali Rattansi
RADIOACTIVITY Claudio Tuniz
RASTAFARI Ennis B. Edmonds
READING Belinda Jack
THE REAGAN REVOLUTION Gil Troy
REALITY Jan Westerhoff
RECONSTRUCTION Allen C. Guelzo
THE REFORMATION Peter Marshall
REFUGEES Gil Loescher
RELATIVITY Russell Stannard
RELIGION Thomas A. Tweed
RELIGION IN AMERICA Timothy Beal
THE RENAISSANCE Jerry Brotton
RENAISSANCE ART
    Geraldine A. Johnson
RENEWABLE ENERGY Nick Jelley
REPTILES T. S. Kemp
REVOLUTIONS Jack A. Goldstone
RHETORIC Richard Toye
RISK Baruch Fischhoff and John Kadvany
RITUAL Barry Stephenson
RIVERS Nick Middleton
ROBOTICS Alan Winfield
ROCKS Jan Zalasiewicz
ROMAN BRITAIN Peter Salway
THE ROMAN EMPIRE
    Christopher Kelly
THE ROMAN REPUBLIC
    David M. Gwynn
ROMANTICISM Michael Ferber
ROUSSEAU Robert Wokler
THE RULE OF LAW Aziz Z. Huq
RUSSELL A. C. Grayling
THE RUSSIAN ECONOMY
    Richard Connolly
RUSSIAN HISTORY Geoffrey Hosking
RUSSIAN LITERATURE
    Catriona Kelly
RUSSIAN POLITICS Brian D. Taylor
THE RUSSIAN REVOLUTION
    S. A. Smith
SAINTS Simon Yarrow
SAMURAI Michael Wert
SAVANNAS Peter A. Furley
SCEPTICISM Duncan Pritchard
SCHIZOPHRENIA Chris Frith and
    Eve Johnstone

SCHOPENHAUER
    Christopher Janaway
SCIENCE AND RELIGION
    Thomas Dixon and Adam R. Shapiro
SCIENCE FICTION David Seed
THE SCIENTIFIC REVOLUTION
    Lawrence M. Principe
SCOTLAND Rab Houston
SECULARISM Andrew Copson
THE SELF Marya Schechtman
SEXUAL SELECTION Marlene Zuk and
    Leigh W. Simmons
SEXUALITY Véronique Mottier
WILLIAM SHAKESPEARE
    Stanley Wells
SHAKESPEARE'S COMEDIES
    Bart van Es
SHAKESPEARE'S SONNETS AND
    POEMS Jonathan F. S. Post
SHAKESPEARE'S TRAGEDIES
    Stanley Wells
GEORGE BERNARD SHAW
    Christopher Wixson
MARY SHELLEY Charlotte Gordon
THE SHORT STORY Andrew Kahn
SIKHISM Eleanor Nesbitt
SILENT FILM Donna Kornhaber
THE SILK ROAD James A. Millward
SLANG Jonathon Green
SLEEP Steven W. Lockley and
    Russell G. Foster
SMELL Matthew Cobb
ADAM SMITH Christopher J. Berry
SOCIAL AND CULTURAL
    ANTHROPOLOGY
    John Monaghan and Peter Just
SOCIALISM Michael Newman
SOCIAL PSYCHOLOGY
    Richard J. Crisp
SOCIAL SCIENCE Alexander Betts
SOCIAL WORK Sally Holland and
    Jonathan Scourfield
SOCIOLINGUISTICS John Edwards
SOCIOLOGY Steve Bruce
SOCRATES C. C. W. Taylor
SOFT MATTER Tom McLeish
SOPHOCLES Edith Hall
SOUND Mike Goldsmith
SOUTHEAST ASIA James R. Rush
THE SOVIET UNION Stephen Lovell

THE SPANISH CIVIL WAR
    Helen Graham
SPANISH LITERATURE Jo Labanyi
THE SPARTANS Andrew J. Bayliss
SPINOZA Roger Scruton
SPIRITUALITY Philip Sheldrake
SPORT Mike Cronin
STARS Andrew King
STATISTICS David J. Hand
STEM CELLS Jonathan Slack
STOICISM Brad Inwood
STRUCTURAL ENGINEERING
    David Blockley
STUART BRITAIN John Morrill
SUBURBS Carl Abbott
THE SUN Philip Judge
SUPERCONDUCTIVITY
    Stephen Blundell
SUPERSTITION Stuart Vyse
SURVEILLANCE David Lyon
SUSTAINABILITY Saleem Ali
SYMBIOSIS Nancy A. Moran
SYMMETRY Ian Stewart
SYNAESTHESIA Julia Simner
SYNTHETIC BIOLOGY
    Jamie A. Davies
SYSTEMS BIOLOGY Eberhard O. Voit
TAXATION Stephen Smith
TEETH Peter S. Ungar
TERRORISM Charles Townshend
THEATRE Marvin Carlson
THEOLOGY David F. Ford
THINKING AND REASONING
    Jonathan St B. T. Evans
THOUGHT Tim Bayne
THUCYDIDES Jennifer T. Roberts
TIBETAN BUDDHISM
    Matthew T. Kapstein
TIDES David George Bowers and
    Emyr Martyn Roberts
TIME Jenann Ismael
TOCQUEVILLE Harvey C. Mansfield
TOLERATION Andrew Murphy
J. R. R. TOLKIEN Matthew Townend
LEO TOLSTOY Liza Knapp
TOPOLOGY Richard Earl
TRAGEDY Adrian Poole
TRANSLATION Matthew Reynolds
THE TREATY OF VERSAILLES
    Michael S. Neiberg

TRIGONOMETRY
   Glen Van Brummelen
THE TROJAN WAR Eric H. Cline
ANTHONY TROLLOPE Dinah Birch
TRUST Katherine Hawley
THE TUDORS John Guy
TWENTIETH-CENTURY BRITAIN
   Kenneth O. Morgan
TYPOGRAPHY Paul Luna
THE UNITED NATIONS
   Jussi M. Hanhimäki
UNIVERSITIES AND COLLEGES
   David Palfreyman and Paul Temple
THE U.S. CIVIL WAR Louis P. Masur
THE U.S. CONGRESS Donald A. Ritchie
THE U.S. CONSTITUTION
   David J. Bodenhamer
THE U.S. SUPREME COURT
   Linda Greenhouse
UTILITARIANISM
   Katarzyna de Lazari-Radek and
   Peter Singer
UTOPIANISM Lyman Tower Sargent
VATICAN II Shaun Blanchard and
   Stephen Bullivant
VETERINARY SCIENCE
   James Yeates
THE VICTORIANS Martin Hewitt
THE VIKINGS Julian D. Richards
VIOLENCE Philip Dwyer

THE VIRGIN MARY
   Mary Joan Winn Leith
THE VIRTUES Craig A. Boyd and
   Kevin Timpe
VIRUSES Dorothy H. Crawford
VOLCANOES Michael J. Branney and
   Jan Zalasiewicz
VOLTAIRE Nicholas Cronk
WAR AND RELIGION
   Jolyon Mitchell and Joshua Rey
WAR AND TECHNOLOGY
   Alex Roland
WATER John Finney
WAVES Mike Goldsmith
WEATHER Storm Dunlop
SIMONE WEIL
   A. Rebecca Rozelle-Stone
THE WELFARE STATE David Garland
WITCHCRAFT Malcolm Gaskill
WITTGENSTEIN A. C. Grayling
WORK Stephen Fineman
WORLD MUSIC Philip Bohlman
WORLD MYTHOLOGY David Leeming
THE WORLD TRADE
   ORGANIZATION Amrita Narlikar
WORLD WAR II Gerhard L. Weinberg
WRITING AND SCRIPT
   Andrew Robinson
ZIONISM Michael Stanislawski
ÉMILE ZOLA Brian Nelson

Available soon:

GEORGE ELIOT Juliette Atkinson
MATHEMATICAL BIOLOGY
   Philip Maini
AGATHA CHRISTIE Gill Plain

HUMAN GEOGRAPHY
   Patricia Daley and Ian Klinke
JORGE LUIS BORGES Ilan Stavans
MOSES MAIMONIDES Ross Brann

For more information visit our website

www.oup.com/vsi/

Joshua Landy

MARCEL PROUST

A Very Short Introduction

OXFORD
UNIVERSITY PRESS

Oxford University Press is a department of the University of Oxford.
It furthers the University's objective of excellence in research, scholarship,
and education by publishing worldwide. Oxford is a registered trade mark of
Oxford University Press in the UK and in certain other countries.

Published in the United States of America by Oxford University Press
198 Madison Avenue, New York, NY 10016, United States of America.

Library of Congress Cataloging-in-Publication Data
Names: Landy, Joshua, 1965- author.
Title: Marcel Proust : a very short introduction / Joshua Landy.
Other titles: World according to Proust
Description: New York, NY : Oxford University Press, 2024. |
Series: Very short introductions | "Published in hardcover as The World
According to Proust in 2023" | Includes bibliographical references and index.
Identifiers: LCCN 2024001962 (print) | LCCN 202400 (ebook) |
ISBN 9780197586556 (paperback) | ISBN 9780197586570 (epub)
Subjects: LCSH: Proust, Marcel, 1871–1922. À la recherche du temps pe
Classification: LCC PQ2631.R63 A82776 2024 (print) | LCC PQ2631.R63
(ebook) | DDC 843/.912—dc23/eng/20240117
LC record available at https://lccn.loc.gov/2024001962
LC ebook record available at https://lccn.loc.gov/2024001963

Integrated Books International, United States of America

Contents

List of illustrations xvii

List of abbreviations xix

Acknowledgments xxi

Preface xxiii

1 Art and life 1

2 Plot and character 9

3 Memories and impressions 17

4 Love and sex 26

5 Knowledge and ignorance 42

6 Inclusion and exclusion 55

7 Art and artists 62

8 Intellect and intuition 78

9   True self and total self   83

10   Why a novel?   101

A postscript for diehard Proust fans: Does the narrator write *In Search of Lost Time*?   115

References   119

Further reading   131

Index   135

Marcel Proust

List of illustrations

1 *Little Miss Sunshine* **xxiv**
   © 2006 Twentieth Century Fox.
   Written by Michael Arndt.
   All rights reserved

2 Photograph of Marcel
   Proust **3**
   Hulton Archive/Getty Images

3 "House of Aunt Léonie" **5**
   DIDIER FOTO/Shutterstock

4 *Monty Python's Flying
   Circus* **10**
   DVD screen-capture

5 Writer's block **11**
   A la recherche du temps perdu,
   volume 1, de Stéphane Heuet, d'après
   l'œuvre de Marcel Proust, © 1998
   Editions DELCOURT

6 Piazza San Marco **18**
   Photo courtesy of the author

7 Salmon, cilantro, cinnamon,
   scallop **23**
   © Photoongraphy/Shutterstock,
   © azure1/Shutterstock, © Yeti studio/
   Shutterstock, © KPixMining/
   Shutterstock

8 What we can know and how **52**

9 *Un mardi, soirée chez
   Madeleine Lemaire*, Henri
   Gervex, circa 1910 **57**
   Musée Carnavalet, Histoire de Paris

10 A manuscript page from
   Proust's novel **71**
   Bibliothèque nationale de France

11 Art and insight **76**

12 Still-life paintings **114**
   À la recherche du temps perdu,
   volume 3, de Stéphane Heuet, d'après
   l'œuvre de Marcel Proust, © 2002
   Editions DELCOURT

List of abbreviations

The seven volumes of *In Search of Lost Time*

Swann's Way, translated by C. K. Scott Moncrieff, Terence
   Kilmartin, and D. J. Enright. New York: Modern Library,
   1992. (Abbreviated as *S*)

Within a Budding Grove, translated by C. K. Scott Moncrieff,
   Terence Kilmartin, and D. J. Enright. New York: Modern
   Library, 1992. (Abbreviated as *BG*)

The Guermantes Way, translated by C. K. Scott Moncrieff, Terence
   Kilmartin, and D. J. Enright. New York: Modern Library,
   1993. (Abbreviated as *GW*)

Sodom and Gomorrah, translated by C. K. Scott Moncrieff,
   Terence Kilmartin, and D. J. Enright. New York: Modern
   Library, 1993. (Abbreviated as *SG*)

The Captive, in *The Captive and The Fugitive*, translated by
   C. K. Scott Moncrieff, Terence Kilmartin, and D. J. Enright.
   New York: Modern Library, 1993. (Abbreviated as *C*)

The Fugitive, in *The Captive and The Fugitive*, translated by
   C. K. Scott Moncrieff, Terence Kilmartin, and D. J. Enright.
   New York: Modern Library, 1993. (Abbreviated as *F*)

Time Regained, translated by D. J. Enright, Terence Kilmartin,
   and Andreas Mayor. New York: Modern Library, 1993.
   (Abbreviated as *TR*)

Other works by Proust mentioned in this book

Le Carnet de 1908. Paris: Gallimard, 1976. (Abbreviated as *1908*)

By Way of Sainte-Beuve, translated by Sylvia Townsend Warner. London: Hogarth Press, 1984. (Abbreviated as *BSB*)

Essais et articles. Paris: Gallimard, 1994. (Abbreviated as *EA*)

Le mystérieux correspondant et autres nouvelles inédites. Paris: Editions de Fallois, 2019. (Abbreviated as *MC*)

Marcel Proust on Art and Literature, translated by Sylvia Townsend Warner. New York: Carroll & Graf, 1984. (Abbreviated as *MPAL*)

Matinée chez la Princesse de Guermantes: Cahiers du "Temps retrouvé." Paris: Gallimard, 1982. (Abbreviated as *MPG*)

On Reading Ruskin, translated by Jean Autret, William Burford, and Phillip J. Wolfe. New Haven, CT: Yale University Press, 1987. (Abbreviated as *ORR*)

Note: translations from *1908*, *EA*, and *MC* are my own. On occasion I have modified translations in *S*, *BG*, *GW*, *SG*, *C*, *F*, and *TR*, drawing on the original French in *À la recherche du temps perdu* (Paris: Gallimard, 1987–88).

Acknowledgments

When Oxford University Press asked me to write a Very Short Introduction, the invitation came as a delightful surprise; I felt, and still feel, extremely honored to be included in this fantastic series. My first thought was of the French knight in *Monty Python and the Holy Grail*: do people really need another book from me on Proust? They've already got one! (If only it were "verra nahsse," to quote that same John Cleese character.) But I eventually came around, and I'm so glad I did.

I wrote much of what follows during a year at the Stanford Humanities Center; many thanks to the Center, to its excellent director Roland Greene, and to its wonderful staff. I am also deeply grateful to Dan Edelstein—the Title Whisperer—as well as to R. Lanier Anderson, Erin Carlston, Pardis Dabashi, Katie Ebner-Landy, Kate Elkins, Gary Kemp, Ian Miller, Alexander Nehamas, Richard Neer, Thomas Pavel, Sarah G. Peterson, Robert Pippin, Jeremy Sabol, Richard Terdiman, Richard Zuckerman, and Karen Zumhagen-Yekplé for all of their advice, assistance, encouragement, and kindness.

I couldn't possibly have hoped for more generous anonymous readers; their excellent suggestions have left many traces in the end result. Above all, I owe an incalculable debt to Elisabeth Ladenson, who read every word; commented expertly, magnanimously, and profusely; and bore with me as I asked endless questions.

Finally, a special word of appreciation to the incredible students from Proust classes spanning more than two decades, both at Stanford and in Chicago. You have made my working life a source of never-ending joy.

Preface

Marcel Proust may well be France's best-known literary writer. He lived only fifty-one years—from 1871 to 1922—but managed in that short span to write stories, essays, translations, and a 3,000-page, 7-volume book, *In Search of Lost Time* (1913–27), that some people have called the world's greatest novel. (Those people may include me.) It took him thirteen years, and he died before being able to revise some of the later volumes, with the result that a dead character will occasionally come back to life; but it is finished enough to count as one of the all-time masterpieces of European literature.

Proust's writing has had an impact not only on literature but also on thought: in their very different ways, philosophers Walter Benjamin, Gilles Deleuze, Maurice Merleau-Ponty, Derek Parfit, and Paul Ricoeur all drew inspiration from him. So did theorists of narrative like Gérard Genette. Empirical psychologists have done studies on the phenomenon of involuntary memory, and it's rare to see such a study that does not cite Proust. (A 2013 paper titled "Involuntary Autobiographical Memories," by Rosemary Bradley et al., has a large picture of madeleines and tea at the top.)

When Virginia Woolf read the *Search*, she wrote to Roger Fry asking "what remains to be written after that?" Samuel Beckett, Anaïs Nin, Carlos Fuentes, Harold Pinter, James Merrill,

and Anne Carson were all influenced by Proust; so were
filmmakers like Jean-Luc Godard, Chris Marker, Luchino
Visconti, and (arguably) Alfred Hitchcock.

There are films based on Proust's novel, as well as a French TV
adaptation that is surprisingly good. There's also a graphic novel
version that is sublime; you'll see images from it in this book. In
2019, a fan embarked on an out-loud reading of the entire novel
(in French) in San Francisco subway stations. People keep
writing more and more biographies of Proust, many of them
very long.

Monty Python hilariously imagined a "Summarise Proust"
competition. In Wes Anderson's *The Life Aquatic*, Cate Blanchett
reads Proust to her unborn child. And the 2006 comedy *Little Miss
Sunshine* features Steve Carell as "the number one Proust scholar in
the United States." (Yes, my friends do ask me. And no, I wish!)

1. Proust shows up not just in philosophy books and in psychology
studies, but also in popular films such as *Little Miss Sunshine*. The
scene pictured here goes over particularly well with fans of Proust,
thanks to this memorable bit of dialogue:

Frank (Steve Carell):   "Larry Sugarman is perhaps the second most
                        highly regarded Proust scholar in the US."
Rich (Greg Kinnear):   "Who's number 1?"
Frank: "That would be me, Rich."

There is excellent reason for all of this interest. Part of it has to do with the revolution in style Proust undertook (everything infinitely long, infinitely complex, and yet also carefully organized). And part of it has to do with the series of brilliant observations and difficult questions raised by his writing: how we can feel at home in the world; how we can find genuine connection with other human beings; how we can find enchantment in a world without God; how art can transform our lives; whether an artist's life can shed light on her work; what we can know about the world, other people, and ourselves; when not knowing is better than knowing; how sexual orientation affects questions of connection and identity; who we really are, deep down; what memory tells us about our inner world; why it might be good to think of our life as a story; how we can feel like a single, unified person when we are torn apart by competing desires and change over time; and why it matters to read Proust's writing itself, not just this book, even if I don't do a terrible job.

That's quite a lot to talk about in a hundred-odd pages, and unfortunately I won't get to all kinds of other things I love in Proust: the character Françoise (and her fascinating way of speaking), modern technology, habit, etymology, symbolic geography, metaphysics, "metonymic metaphor," the magic of names, the complicated relationship to Henri Bergson, the (partial) love of discontinuity... But the themes in the previous paragraph are the kind Proust focused on when he discussed his book, so it doesn't seem totally unfair, for a short (*very* short!) introduction, to focus on those.

From time to time, I'll refer to Proust's articles, his letters, an interview he gave, and the prefaces he wrote to his translations of Ruskin; they help us see that Proust agrees with his narrator-protagonist on *some* things, even if he disagrees with him on others. But I won't have much to say about the short stories, the pastiches, or the abandoned early manuscript (published posthumously as *Jean Santeuil*), despite there being some lovely stuff in each. When people say "I'm reading Proust," they usually mean "I'm reading that 3,000-page novel that had better be the masterpiece you promised me it was." I think they're right. And I think it is.

Chapter 1
Art and life

A book like this would normally start with a few pages of biography: it would tell you who Proust's parents were, where he was born, who he dated, what he ate for breakfast, and all kinds of other juicy information. There *is* some juicy information here and there—André Gide took a pass on publishing *Swann's Way* when it was offered to him, and Proust had the last laugh by winning the Goncourt prize in 1919—but there isn't that much of it, and in any case, with apologies to anyone who wanted to hear more of that kind of thing, it isn't what I'm going to focus on. That's partly because biographical information is so readily available online (as well as in some wonderful books), and partly because there's so much else to talk about; but it's mainly because Proust would have disapproved, and I just couldn't look at myself in the mirror if I did it. What I'd rather do instead is explain *why* Proust would have disapproved, because fascinatingly enough, this disapproval ended up generating part of his literary masterpiece, *In Search of Lost Time*.

Why you shouldn't want a biography

Proust was reacting against one of the most prominent critics of the nineteenth century, Charles Augustin Sainte-Beuve. When Sainte-Beuve wrote about the novelists of his age, he didn't just analyze and assess their books; he also talked about what they were like as dinner companions. That, Proust thought, is why Sainte-Beuve ended up getting it wrong about giants like Balzac, Stendhal, Nerval, Flaubert, and Manet. Sainte-Beuve's mistake? "Explaining the true Fantin or Manet, the one that is only found in their work, on the basis of the mortal man" (*EA*, 273–74).

Proust's conclusion was simple but important: it doesn't matter whether a writer is good or bad company. You can be a brilliant artist and a lousy talker, or a dauber with the gift of the gab. You can make great art but not fully understand what you've accomplished (that's what Proust thought about the painter Chardin) or even get it wrong about what you've accomplished (that's what Proust's narrator thinks about the playwright Molière). You can be an unfaithful spouse who writes moralizing fiction, or a faithful spouse who writes libertine fiction. (That's what Proust's narrator thinks about Mme de Genlis and Choderlos de Laclos, respectively.) So what we know about an author's life tells us next to nothing about her novels. In fact, as a famous line in an early Proust manuscript puts it, "a book is the product of a different self from the self we manifest in our habits, in our social life, in our vices" (*BSB*, 76).

This idea is beautifully illustrated in the *Search*, where all three of the great (fictional) artists—Vinteuil the composer, Bergotte the novelist, Elstir the painter—are flawed as people, but "the prudish respectability of the one [Vinteuil], the intolerable defects of the other [Bergotte], even the pretentious vulgarity of an Elstir in his early days...prove nothing against them: their genius is manifested in their works." (The same is true even for doctors, like Cottard: "and we realised that this imbecile was a great physician.") (*TR*, 42; *BG*, 97.)

In fact Proust's own life story is disappointingly lackluster. Arguably the best reason to read it is that it is such great evidence for his own view—Proust the novelist is vastly more interesting than Proust the person!—and that it helps us appreciate the amazing alchemy of art; as Proust scholar Malcolm Bowie said, "that a life like that should have produced a novel like this is the miracle of miracles."

There's something else that follows from Proust's anti-Sainte-Beuvian stance, but that's something I hesitate to mention, in case you happen to have gone to see Proust's bedroom in the Musée Carnavalet or visited the town of Illiers in north-central France.

2. Proust the uninteresting (albeit dapper) person. Proust the fascinating novelist not pictured.

Some years ago Illiers rebranded itself "Illiers-Combray," marketing itself as the town prominently featured in Proust's novel. Proust's protagonist used to spend holidays in Combray as a child, visiting his aunt Léonie, eating madeleines on a Sunday, taking walks near Charles Swann's house or by the Guermantes estate, and so on. But that's Proust's protagonist—a fictional character—and not Proust: Combray isn't a real town, Proust didn't have an aunt Léonie, and Proust almost certainly didn't eat a madeleine that brought back his childhood. So it's a bit odd that you can now visit "Combray" and visit the "Maison de Tante Léonie." Proust would not have liked this. He would have called it "idolatry."

"Idolatry" is a word Proust uses in the preface to *La Bible d'Amiens*, his translation of a book by John Ruskin. Here Proust raises an eyebrow at people who get excited on seeing a dress that's exactly like one worn by a Balzac heroine, or insist on visiting a house Balzac lived in. "Once stripped of the spirit that is in it," Proust writes, the dress "is no more than a sign deprived of its meaning, that is to say, nothing; and to keep on adoring it so much as to be enraptured upon encountering it in real life on a woman's body is, properly speaking, idolatry" (*ORR*, 56). If worshiping physical objects in place of God, the true object of veneration, is religious idolatry, then fetishizing dresses and houses in place of novels, the true object of veneration, is *aesthetic* idolatry. So while it's entirely understandable in a way that fans of Proust eat up biographies (Sainte-Beuvism) and make pilgrimages to so-called "Combray" (idolatry), I fear it all makes Proust turn in his grave in Père-Lachaise. (Don't go there either, by the way.)

To be fair, we probably don't make Proust turn *too* much in that grave of his if we visit him, his bed, or his favorite towns in the right frame of mind. It's fine to go out of curiosity, to pay homage to the great writer that he was, or even to take snarky photos of the "Maison de Tante Léonie," as I myself may possibly have done. We just need to remember that Aunt Léonie wasn't a real person,

3. The so-called "House of Aunt Léonie," in Illiers-Combray. Give it a miss.

that Proust probably never ate a magic madeleine that restored his memories of Illiers, that there's nothing intrinsically special about the seaside town Cabourg, and above all that none of what we see in these places explains in the slightest how the astonishing novel came into being.

Why Proust's novel isn't one either

For Proust, then, the everyday self is entirely different from the writing self, also known as the "true" self. You're quite simply a different person when you make art from when you move around and interact with other people. And that means there's no inference that can be legitimately drawn from your biography to an assessment of your work. In fact, it can be harmful to your work if people know about your life, since they'll be tempted to read all kinds of things into it that aren't really there.

This actually applies quite nicely to Proust's own novel, which many readers have taken to be a lightly fictionalized autobiography. In a way that assumption is understandable, given that Proust is writing in the first person, that he draws on his own experience for a number of the scenes, and that there are two moments in which the character seems to be called "Marcel." Still, some believe that if Proust had lived long enough he would have edited out at least one of those "Marcels," just as he had deleted the occasional stray "Marcel" in previous volumes. And the other of those "Marcels" belongs to one of the all-time great and dizzying sentences in world literature: "Then she would find her tongue and say 'My—' or 'My darling—' followed by my Christian name, which, if we give the narrator the same name as the author of this book, would be 'My Marcel' or 'My darling Marcel'" (*C*, 91). Isn't that fantastic? Far from saying the character's name *is* Marcel, this mind-bending sentence only says it *would* be Marcel, *if* it were the same name as the author's. If Proust's novel were really an autobiography, the question wouldn't even arise.

Proust himself frequently said, to anyone who would listen, that the character isn't him (or at least isn't entirely him). For example, in an interview published in 1913, right before the first volume came out, Proust spoke of "the character who narrates, who says 'I' (and who is not me)" (*EA*, 254). And as it happens, there are some highly significant differences between the two. Not only did Proust (most likely) never eat a madeleine that brought back lost memories; he also never visited a town named Balbec, never met anyone named Guermantes, and never heard a septet by a composer named Vinteuil. (We'll hear more about Balbec, Vinteuil, and the madeleine in due course.) Meanwhile, Proust had a brother; the narrator is an only child. Proust's mother was Jewish; the narrator is all Catholic, and his maternal grandfather is even mildly antisemitic. Proust was gay; the narrator is straight, so straight in fact that same-sex desire seems to baffle him. (More on that in chapter 4.)

Some readers have reacted to the difference in sexual orientation by claiming that the character's love interests—Gilberte Swann, Albertine Simonet, the Duchesse de Guermantes, Alix de Stermaria—are really men in disguise. That hypothesis is not entirely absurd, since Gide reported Proust as saying he had "transposed" some same-sex experiences onto female characters, "Gilberte" and "Albertine" look like men's names with feminine endings, and one or two other small things point in that direction. But a number of features mark Albertine as female, from her physicality (whose difference from his own delights the narrator) to the social taboo around cohabitation (which would not be the case for another man) and the fact that she ultimately tries to coerce the narrator into marriage (gay marriage hardly being a realistic plan, to put it mildly, in the early twentieth century).

Above all, though, turning the women into men would eliminate lesbianism, and lesbianism (along with bisexuality) is vitally important in the novel, where it dramatizes the difficulty of fully understanding another person. (This is an argument made by Elisabeth Ladenson in her brilliant and indispensable book, *Proust's Lesbianism*.) The narrator's desperate struggles to project himself into Albertine's mind, to see the world from her point of view, only reveal to him "the curtain that is forever lowered for other people over what happens in the mysterious intimacy of every human creature" (*F*, 742); the fact that her sexual life is something he cannot even begin to imagine makes this problem cognitively sharp, emotionally powerful, and existentially meaningful.

So we should almost certainly keep the female characters female. Even when we do, fortunately, Proust's novel remains one that is deeply interested in male same-sex desire: the single longest sentence in the novel is a lament for the situation of persecuted gay men like Oscar Wilde. But with the women as women, it also preserves an interest in *female* same-sex desire, as well as in stark versions of the "problem of other minds."

When it comes to Proust's novel, then, reading it as an autobiography makes it a less interesting book. It draws on a life, but its purpose isn't just to retell it; it's to turn those raw materials, together with elements of pure invention, into a stunning work of philosophical fiction, making it something that can have a powerful and lasting effect on each and every one of us. We're about to see why that is.

Chapter 2
Plot and character

It's notoriously hard to boil Proust's 3,000-page novel down to a short synopsis; that's why Monty Python's "All-England Summarise Proust Competition" is so hilarious. At the risk of unintentional comedy, I'll try to give a general sense by focusing on a few central strands. There will be spoilers—but there won't, I hope, be typos. Let's see how I do on the "Proustometer."

My entry for the "Summarise Proust" competition

The main thing to know is that, in spite of its title, this book isn't actually a search for lost time. Yes, the narrator does remember things, and remembering is important, but he's never really *looking* for memory. He also doesn't spend a lot of time saying how sad he is that he's forgotten things. Nor are forgotten memories something you can really "search" for, since they tend to return unbidden. And above all, as we'll see in a moment, the memories themselves are not what truly matters.

So what *does* the narrator go after? Well, he tries (successfully) to enter high society, making increasingly powerful connections with the high-born Guermantes family. He strives (less successfully) for intimate connection, via friendship and love. He spends time with

9

4. Mr. Rutherford from Leicester trying valiantly to score points on the "Proustometer," in Monty Python's "All-England Summarise Proust Competition," from *Monty Python's Flying Circus*, season 3, episode 5 (originally aired November 16, 1972). I like to think the typo—"sweet chear" for "sweet cheat"—is entirely deliberate.

amiable aristocrat Robert de Saint-Loup; has a childhood crush on Gilberte Swann (daughter of family friend Charles Swann); obsesses over the Duchesse de Guermantes; and has a relatively long relationship, troubled by pathological jealousy, with Albertine Simonet.

He also lingers in nature, seeking to decipher the secret language of hawthorns and trees. He visits Balbec (a seaside town in Normandy) and Venice, hoping each time for a transformative change of environment. In quest of aesthetic satisfaction, he reads books by a novelist called Bergotte, admires canvases by a painter called Elstir, and listens to melodies by a composer called Vinteuil. And he struggles to produce a novel of his own, battling a case of writer's block that lasts for decades.

5. Proust's novel, *In Search of Lost Time*, features a main character who desperately wants to become an author but, for the most part, finds himself unable to write. This image is from Stéphane Heuet's graphic novel adaptation of Proust.

None of these things brings him lasting happiness. The time he spends around paintings, novels, and septets is exhilarating but transitory; when it comes to high society, friendship, and love, he loses hope of finding something meaningful in any of them; he gives up, too, on being inspired by travel and nature and, above all, on becoming a writer. As far as he can tell, he simply has no talent for it.

His health also goes into (increased) decline, and he spends "long years" in a sanatorium that doesn't do much good, followed by "a long time" in a different sanatorium that doesn't do much good

either, being "no more successful in curing me than the first."
(*TR* 47, 238) (For those interested in keeping track of chronology, the opening line—"for a long time I used to go to bed early"—refers to *this* point in time, the character's middle age, and not to childhood; childhood is, by now, a distant memory.)

There's one ray of light in this otherwise gloomy period: after he eats a madeleine dipped in tea—something he hasn't done in many years—a powerful feeling of euphoria suddenly washes over him, followed by a flood of forgotten childhood memories. (We'll hear more about that in chapter 3.) But the euphoria is short-lived. When we see him on his way to a high society party in the final volume, having returned from the second sanatorium, he is resigned to a life of superficiality: if he can't become a writer, he may as well waste his time with the snobs. Albertine is long dead. Robert de Saint-Loup has been killed in battle. Méséglise, home to the Swanns, has been destroyed in the War. It seems the race is lost.

But while waiting to be admitted to the party, the narrator experiences a series of madeleine-style memories, all in a row; and this time he manages to figure out what such experiences *mean*, why they confer such bliss. The ensuing train of thought ends up solving the problems that have kept him from his vocation, and by the end he's begun work on a novel—one that may or may not be the novel we've just read. (Want to know what I think? See the Postscript.) He has found, amazingly, what he was searching for all along.

Finding identity, connection, and belonging

We're almost done with the "summarise Proust" section of this book, but not quite. The central plot of Proust's novel is indeed about the discovery of a vocation—the narrator becoming a writer, finding a reason for being, finally becoming able to live a meaningful and valuable life—but there's more to it than just that. His quest is also for identity, connection, and belonging.

Identity: after years spent fretting about how difficult it is to know oneself, and how difficult it is even to be a self in the first place, he now has a pretty clear sense of who he is, of what makes him special—sometimes in a good way, sometimes not so much—and of how the episodes in his life can form a single story, instead of reducing him to a heap of fragments. (More about this in chapter 9.)

Connection: like many of us, he longs for a meeting of minds, an encounter where you see another person for who they really are, maybe even fusing with them for a moment, seeing the world, thrillingly, through a different pair of eyes. But unlike many of us, he doesn't find this in friendship or in love, and it's art that, surprisingly, will ride to his eventual rescue. (More on that in chapter 7.)

Belonging: here the question is how we can feel at home in the world, given that almost nothing we encounter is there for our benefit, and indeed much of it positively resists us. One central example in the novel is a first night in an unfamiliar hotel room, where the narrator has a really tough time adjusting to his new surroundings, surroundings that are completely indifferent to him as an individual.

The obvious solution, of course, is simply to get used to things. Over time you stop noticing the "insolent indifference of the clock," the "strange and pitiless" mirror, and the "hostility of the violet curtains." (*S*, 8) But habit is a two-edged sword: it may increase your comfort level, but it does so by placing a barrier between you and the world, preventing you from making authentic contact with what's really there. So how can you genuinely experience reality while still feeling at home within it?

How can you find comfort—a sense of fit between you and everything around you—without walling yourself off in fantasyland?

In Proust's novel, a fascinating answer is available between the lines. That answer? Make art.

Imagine your closest friends sitting in a circle around a bowl of flowers, all doing their best to paint a picture of it. Each of those paintings is going to turn out slightly different, because each of them is going to bear the mark of its creator; yet each of them is presumably going to feature flowers. So these paintings will make contact with reality while, at the same time, reflecting the unique qualities of your friends. The flowers become *their* flowers, imprinted with their subjectivity. It is their personal style—but with the world's objects still visible beneath. That's how art can tame the world, bringing it under your spell, making it conform to your special way of seeing. That's how it can allow you to feel at home.

We saw a moment ago that the narrator solves the connection problem by experiencing the art of others; now we can add that he solves the belonging problem by making art of his own. High society, travel, and friendship haven't done much for him at all. Love and nature have inadvertently shone a clarifying light on his character, but they haven't delivered the connection and enchantment he was hoping for. What really transforms his life is art. Thanks to the magic of individual style, art is the place where we can enter most deeply into the soul of another person—and also where self and world meet and shake hands, where each of us can finally find ourselves in harmony with the cosmos.

Re-enchanting the world

So the narrator ends up not just with a vocation—a meaningful purpose, a reason for living—but also with identity, connection, and belonging; he has a self he can point to, a conduit he can use to other minds, and a world he can feel at home in. All that is true, but there's something else he achieves, and it may well be more important than the rest put together. That something is enchantment.

Aristocrats, hawthorns, Albertine, Venice: everywhere he goes, the narrator is powerfully drawn to people, places, and things that appear to promise a special kind of experience. In every case it feels as though he can enter a mysterious, hidden realm, a world within our world. That realm has its own "laws," laws that make it both internally consistent and different from the reality we know. It is walled off from us, beyond the probing of our senses—but there's a secret passageway allowing us to make contact with it.

That's precisely what the narrator ends up discovering after all his years in the wilderness of insipid society, fruitless friendship, and failed romance. Thanks to memory, nature, and love, he finds a hidden world within himself, a consistent yet unique set of psychological laws; thanks to art, he detects analogous worlds within a host of other people. The universe lights up in a blaze of solar systems: the Elstir system, the Vinteuil system, the Vermeer system, the Dostoevsky system…

It's probably no coincidence that the narrator first falls in love with hawthorns in a church, and it may not be a coincidence that madeleine and tea are so reminiscent of wine and wafer: what Proust's narrator ultimately receives is a secular version of everything promised by Christianity. The world now contains pockets of mystery and wonder, a dimension transcending the visible, and hidden depths beneath everyday surfaces; we're granted access to it in epiphanic moments of revelation; that access feels like a miracle, given how hard it is to know other people; and the form it takes is a new infinity, as the sum of all artists past, present, and future. "Thanks to art, instead of seeing

15

one world only, our own, we see that world multiply itself and we have at our disposal as many worlds as there are original artists, worlds more different one from the other than those which revolve in infinite space." (*TR*, 299) A desolate cosmos bursts back into life.

Chapter 3
Memories and impressions

But let's start filling all of that in, beginning with what Proust is best known for: his fascinating account of involuntary memory. This account is the reason they're still selling so many madeleines at "Illiers-Combray." (Though remember, Proust probably never ate a madeleine that reminded him of his childhood; only his fictional character did that. Oh, and Proust wasn't the first to notice involuntary memory, either—it's the use his novel puts it to that's intriguing.)

Involuntary memory

So what exactly is involuntary memory, and why does it matter? Well, try this: think about what you did on your last birthday. Who was there? What presents did you get? How did it go?

OK, now try this: pick a song you used to listen to a lot a long time ago (the more the better, and the longer the better) but you haven't heard in years. Turn down the lights and listen to it. What comes back to you?

6. A voluntary memory is like a photograph. (If you traveled to Venice in the 1950s and saw the Piazza San Marco, as my uncle did, you might remember it something like this.) Involuntary memories, however, are like a time machine.

Whatever you remembered about your birthday party you remembered voluntarily: you deliberately called it to mind. But whatever you remembered about New Year's Eve twenty years ago, when you made a fool of yourself in front of the person you most cared about while that song was playing—well, that came to you unbidden. (You're welcome.)

Here's how involuntary memory works, according to Proust's narrator. First you have an experience, like making a fool of yourself at a party or spending time with your Aunt Léonie on Sunday mornings. (As the second example shows, the experience can be a repeated one.) While you're having the experience, something is going on in the sensory background: you are hearing a song, say, or tasting some tea and cake. Over time you forget the experience, because your conscious mind doesn't need it for its practical purposes. (It's something that "our intellect, having no use for it, had rejected." (*BG*, 300)) And you also stop listening to the song.

18

So that memory gets sealed in a little jar, preserved intact until the day, perhaps many years later, when you happen to hear the music or eat the cake again—at which point it all comes flooding back. It returns in full force, revealing even more of itself than you noticed at the time, being too busy or preoccupied to take it in.

But it's not just that you remember your great-aunt, her room, and the town around them. You also remember being *you*—the you of twenty years ago. And you remember that you from within: you *become* your past self, wanting what you wanted then, fearing what you feared then, reddening with the shame of what you did then. You feel again, with pain, your love for a person who broke your heart, because it's not just the dry summary you standardly give yourself ("we were together, then split up") but instead the full feeling of the time. A voluntary memory is like a photograph; involuntary memories are like a time machine.

And a third thing happens, more important than both of the others: "the true self...is awakened" (*TR*, 264). There's a part of you that *hasn't* changed in twenty years, a part that is "outside time." ("Outside time" here means "consistent throughout a life," not "immortal.") Something in you experiences "Tangled Up in Blue," or cake and tea, in exactly the same way at a distance of two decades. That something is your true self.

This discovery is life-changing for the narrator, for reasons we'll see in chapter 9. For now, let's just say this: the really amazing thing about involuntary memory isn't that it brings back scenes you'd long forgotten, or even that it brings back a version of you that's been dead for years; it's that it gives you...yourself.

Not nostalgia

But isn't this really just "nostalgia"? Isn't it just the warm fuzzies some soft-hearted people get when they remember the "good old days," days that probably weren't even that good to begin with?

No, I don't think so. To understand that, it helps to recognize what *isn't* making the narrator blissfully happy every time he remembers in this way. First of all, it's not the catalyst of the experience that makes him happy—it's not, for example, that he'd forgotten how delicious madeleines are, and is now rediscovering that. In the *Search*, many of the catalysts are either unexciting (the clink of a spoon hitting a plate) or frankly unpleasant (the smell of gasoline, the "disagreeable sound" of a radiator (*GW*, 474)).

Second, it's not necessarily the content of the recollection. Yes, some of the memories are happy ones (the Piazza San Marco, sunset before dinner...), but others are painful (one involves a desperate feeling of talentlessness), and many are simply drab. Thus the musty odor of a public convenience reminds the narrator of his Uncle Adolphe's sitting room, and he wonders "why the recollection of so trivial an impression had filled me with such happiness" (*BG*, 91). But it's precisely because it's so trivial that it worked: if it had been significant, he'd never have forgotten it. "What best reminds us of a person is precisely what we had forgotten (because it was of no importance, and we therefore left it in full possession of its strength)" (*BG*, 300).

Why does involuntary memory delight us so much, then? Not because the past was better (that New Year's Eve? no way!); not because we imagine it, with the rose-tinted glasses of age, as having been better; but because it drops us back into our old skin, and above all because it shows us something that never changed. It reminds us of events we've forgotten, allows us to become again a long-lost version of ourselves, and reveals a part of us that's always around, all for one brief but magical instant.

In the last volume of Proust's novel, a storm of involuntary memories, one after the other, finally sets the narrator on the path to writing. Understandably, some critics have wondered how plausible this is; all of us have involuntary memories, but few of us see such memories as particularly important, and even fewer of us become writers as a result. Luckily, involuntary memory isn't the only thing that sets the narrator on his way. There's more to come.

Impressions

We just saw how involuntary memory gives a glimpse of a special element within us, a "true self" that stays constant throughout our life, no matter what else changes. But involuntary memory doesn't indicate what that true self *is*, let alone what it contains—the specific ways, that is, in which your true self differs from mine. (We'll hear why such differences *matter* in chapters 7 and 9.)

That's where "impressions" come in (and, as we'll see later, love, language, and art too). Although some readers of Proust have run impressions together with involuntary memories, the two are very different; the narrator makes a clear distinction between them, talking about sensations that come "not from a memory but from an impression" (*C*, 505). The madeleine brings back Combray; the musty toilet, Adolphe's room; some uneven paving stones, Venice; a boot, his late grandmother; but no memory is involved when the narrator finds himself inspired by hawthorns, cornflowers, apple trees, pear trees, pebbles, or clouds. Something else lies "behind" them, as he puts it (*S*, 257). But what?

We get an implicit answer to that question when the narrator recounts his most fruitful "impression," that of the steeples at Martinville. He's on a moving carriage, looking at three spires which, from his vantage point, appear to move around, as though they were animate creatures. He senses there's something to be said about them, and for once in his life he actually says it, dashing down a little prose poem about the scene. And that prose poem adds something crucial to the description: a series of comparisons. In full sunlight, it says, the steeples look like "three birds perched upon the plain"; at sunset, they are "three flowers painted upon the sky"; in the dark, they resemble "three maidens in a legend."

Those are beautiful similes—and also quite quirky. If *you* saw some steeples from a moving car, would a trio of legendary maidens be the first thing that came to your mind? It certainly wouldn't to mine! So what the prose poem captures is not some objective (or "intersubjective") truth about steeples but instead the way they appear to a specific individual. It reveals something about the narrator's psychology. It gives us a measure of how much his mind inflects the world it perceives, the "index of refraction" between his imagination and reality. In other words, it's a window into his *perspective*. That's how the sight of steeples at sunset, and any number of other "impressions," can start to fill in the details of a true self whose existence was indicated by involuntary memory.

A personal perspective

Marcel Proust

Each one of us has a unique perspective like this, an idiosyncratic way of perceiving the world, a framework through which everything we experience is filtered. It's not that we can't see the steeples for what they are—we know perfectly well that they're steeples—but we instinctively compare them, at the same time, to something else. We put them into categories that are partly shared and partly special to us.

By way of illustration, consider the following four objects: salmon, cilantro, cinnamon, scallop. If you had to break them into two pairs, which would go with which?

My guess is that you said salmon goes with scallop (creatures that live in water), and cilantro goes with cinnamon (plants that go on your food). If you did, congratulations: you are a normal, healthy, well-adjusted person—unlike me. For me, it's absolutely and immediately obvious that cilantro goes with scallops, since both of them are utterly revolting when consumed. I don't even have to think about it; the reaction is instantaneous. My way of organizing things is a little bit... well, special.

22

7. Salmon, cilantro, cinnamon, scallop. How would you break them into two pairs of two?

That, I think, is what's going on in the steeples passage, too. The assumption behind it is that we take the stuff in the world and organize it into categories, by isolating key features that certain objects have in common. (For example, some objects are "yum," and some are "yuck.") Sometimes those are features that everyone would agree on, but sometimes they're idiosyncratic to me or you. It's a law of my perspective—and not your perspective—that cilantro goes with scallop. To me, cilantro is like scallop, just as, to Proust's narrator, steeples are like maidens. For him, steeples are connected to women and to nature because, for him, nature and love hold out the promise of replacing religion, of being the pathway to a magical realm within the world but hidden from everyday sight; for me, steeples are like rockets, because of a juvenile infatuation with space travel.

So one good way to learn about who you are is, surprisingly enough, to look outside yourself. Take a peek at the things in the world, see how they speak to you, and contrast that with the way they speak to everyone else, the common denominator of the way we all see them. If you compare an apple by Cézanne, an apple by O'Keeffe, and an apple by Magritte, you get a pretty decent sense of who each of them is. Just look hard enough at apples (or steeples), and maybe you'll find yourself.

The inner life

But still—the way you see apples, the way I see apples, the way Cézanne sees apples: aren't we all just *wrong*? Isn't there a single true thing an apple *really is*, making it frivolous for Magritte to stick one on a face? Isn't the inner life just error?

There's a lovely moment when the narrator starts to entertain exactly this doubt. Having agonized over his long, complicated, tormented relationship with Albertine for hundreds of pages, he suddenly comes to wonder whether the entire thing hasn't, in the end, been something completely banal. "I've been dreaming, the matter is quite simple. I am an indecisive young man, and it is a case of one of those marriages as to which it takes time to find out whether they will happen or not. There is nothing in this peculiar to Albertine" (C, 490). Things only *looked* special from within; to any neutral observer, the situation is totally typical. The narrator's excitement and sufferings, likewise, all make sense from the inside, but are ridiculous from the outside. It's the difference between walking hand in hand with the person you love and watching legions of couples walk hand in hand on a busy beach.

The professional cynics out there (literature departments are well stocked with them) would immediately conclude that, yes, the outside view is the truth and the inside view an illusion. But Proust's narrator isn't so simple-minded. "One can of course reduce everything," he continues,

> to the most commonplace item of newspaper gossip. From outside, it is perhaps thus that I myself would look at it. But I know very

Marcel Proust

24

well that what is true, what at least is also true, is everything that I have thought, what I have read in Albertine's eyes, the fears that torment me, the problem that I continually put to myself with regard to Albertine. The story of the hesitating bridegroom and the broken engagement may correspond to this, as the report of a theatrical performance made by an intelligent reporter may give us the subject of one of Ibsen's plays. But there is something beyond those facts that are reported. (*C*, 490)

If you've ever been in love, you know for yourself that this is correct: even if you were superficially like other couples, your inner states were more than just a repetition of a billion predecessors. Just as the synopsis of a play barely scratches the surface, neither does the plot summary of your life remotely do it justice. "An observer who sees things only from without," says the narrator, "sees nothing" (*S*, 555). Yes, we're often wrong about our states of mind—but not always. And all of our joys are contained in the way things feel from within. The way things feel from within can be every bit as real, and every bit as important, as what can be seen from without.

Chapter 4
Love and sex

Here's a two-part question for those who have read the *Swann in Love* section of *In Search of Lost Time*. (I'm going to borrow both the question and the analysis from a brilliant essay by Hervé Picherit.) When does Charles Swann first fall in love with Odette de Crécy, and for what reason? When, and how, does his mild physical interest in her change into something deeper, more intense, more enduring, more all-consuming? (If you want to play along and keep yourself honest, maybe write your answers down on a scrap of paper—itself very Proustian—and don't peek ahead.)

Love: The official story

I'll come back to these questions a little later in the chapter. For now let me say what the standard story is about love in Proust: it's a downer. There's no special someone that completes you; instead pretty much anyone can do, and whoever it is will torment you. You *think* the person you're with is unique, and that it's her special qualities that make you love her. (I'm using feminine pronouns here because the majority of love-talk in the novel is about female love interests of the narrator, though the standard story also applies to the same-sex relationship between Charlie Morel and the Baron de Charlus.) You think your love for her is "absolutely necessary and predestined" (*GW*, 539), because she is she and because you are you, which means that the two of you belong together. You think you need to be with this person; nobody else could replace her. But every part of this is mistaken.

The reality, according to many statements in the novel, is that love objects are "interchangeable instruments of a pleasure that is always the same" (*S*, 221). Your feelings are not an objective response to something you've found in the other person but just the expression of something subjective in you, something that remains identical regardless of who you're with. What you're looking for is not this particular person but a "world" she appears to give access to, a mysterious domain that allows you to "escap[e] from yourself" (*S*, 222) and journey to somewhere magical. Thus love always goes beyond its object, and has nothing really to do with her properties, which you can't see behind your projections: "our nature…almost creates the women we love, down to their very faults" (*BG*, 218). Instead "the most exclusive love for a person is always a love for something else" (*BG*, 563).

That "something else" can take a number of different forms. In the case of the Duchesse de Guermantes, it's a collection of legendary ancestors. In the case of Gilberte, it's the great writer Bergotte: "had I not loved Gilberte herself principally because she had appeared to me haloed with that aureole of being the friend of Bergotte, of going to look at cathedrals with him?" (*BG*, 512) And in the case of Albertine, it's the essence of a place. "I cannot say whether it was the desire for Balbec or for her that took possession of me then; perhaps my desire for her was itself a lazy, cowardly, and incomplete form of possessing Balbec" (*GW*, 480).

Part of what makes this picture of love so demoralizing is that it means you can never fall in love with someone who (clearly) loves you back. ("One only loves that in which one pursues the inaccessible, one only loves what one does not possess" (*C*, 517). Pretty grim!) One reason is that, as we've seen, you fall in love with a vision your imagination cooked up, a vision that has, at best, a tenuous connection with the actual person.

27

And imagination requires distance to do its work; as soon as you get too close, you see the other person for who they really are, at which point "they are only themselves, that is to say next to nothing" (*C*, 116). So you only want what you can't have, or at best what you think you can't have. The other person has to seem unapproachable, unavailable, uninterested—maybe not even into your entire gender.

If a relationship somehow manages to start, the only thing that can keep it going is jealousy, for exactly the same reason. Familiarity breeds boredom, but should you be lucky enough to have a partner with a wandering eye, hey presto, the distance and the magic are back. "Behind each of her words, [we] feel that a lie is lurking, behind each house to which she says that she has gone, another house, behind each action, each person, another action, another person.... All this confronts the sensitive intellectual with a universe full of depths which his jealousy longs to plumb and which are not without interest to his intelligence" (*F*, 836). And if—even better—she's attracted to people of her own sex, suddenly she belongs once again to a mysterious world.

When you put all this together, love turns out to be an illusion— the illusion that you appreciate someone for her unique qualities, and that the bond between you is objective and necessary—and therefore hollow, pointless, meaningless. ("Nullity of love, which, pre-existent and mobile, comes to rest at the image of a woman simply because that woman will be almost impossible of attainment" (*BG*, 597).) It's also a *painful* illusion, a situation that guarantees you will never get what you want, that your loves will be either short-lived or racked with jealousy, and that you will always be unhappy. Desire invariably "forces one to love what will make one suffer" (*F*, 825). The only choice is "to cease from suffering or to cease from loving" (*C*, 113); love is "an incurable malady" (*C*, 105), something bad for you, to be avoided if at all possible. If you see someone attractive, run and hide.

Love: The reality

Are you properly discouraged? I hope so. But here's the thing: that hard-bitten, Gauloise-smoking theory of love doesn't entirely hold up. There's a lovely moment in the second volume when the narrator talks about Gabrielle Elstir, wife of the great painter. Why did Elstir fall in love with her? Why is he *still* in love with her? Here's why:

> I understood then that to a certain ideal type illustrated by certain lines, certain arabesques which reappeared incessantly throughout his work, to a certain canon of art, he had attributed a character that was almost divine…[But] he had never been able to look at it with detachment, to extract emotion from it, until the day on which he encountered it, realized outside himself, in the body of a woman, the body of the woman who had in due course become Mme Elstir and in whom he had been able…to find it meritorious, moving, divine. (*BG*, 685-7)

Here's a relationship that has lasted decades and that seems very happy. There's no indication that jealousy is involved. And it's clearly based on a positive emotion, namely admiration of beauty. There are other relationships in the novel, too, that don't seem to be toxic: the narrator's father and mother, for all the quibbles that make them a normal married couple, seem to be doing just fine, and we have no reason to think that Mme de Villeparisis is tormenting the Baron de Norpois with the burning fires of jealousy.

In fact, the narrator himself seems to admit once or twice that his ostensibly universal rules only apply to him: "thus already they were acting upon me, those influences which recur in the course of our successive love-affairs…*or which at least have recurred in the course of mine*" (*BG*, 562). At most, maybe, these rules apply to people in his psychological category, which is to say "all those who have too little confidence in themselves to believe that a woman can ever fall in love with them" (*SG*, 308-9), "all those people whose self-analysis outweighs their self-esteem" (*SG*, 310). People like Swann, Charlus, Robert de Saint-Loup—but not people like Elstir, Norpois, or his own mother.

Now that we think about it—do these so-called laws of love even apply reliably to *him*? Not so much! When he gets smitten with the Duchesse de Guermantes, it's because she *smiles* at him: "and at once I fell in love with her, for if it is sometimes enough to make us love a woman that she should look on us with contempt, as I supposed Mlle Swann to have done, and that we should think that she can never be ours, sometimes, too, it is enough that she should look on us kindly, as Mme de Guermantes was doing, and that we should think of her as almost ours already" (*S*, 250-1). Elsewhere, he says that if he'd known Andrée liked him, "it is perhaps with Andrée that I would have fallen in love" (*C*, 16). And when Albertine writes "I like you" on a pad of paper, "I said to myself that it was with her that I would have my romance" (*BG*, 675). Given everything we've seen above, this is amazing. Confidence doesn't reduce interest; it increases it!

Conversely, when Albertine rebuffs an attempted kiss, "my dreams abandoned her, once they had ceased to be nourished by the hope of a possession of which I had supposed them to be independent" (*BG*, 702). Whatever happened to the claim that "to release...those agonies which prepare the way for love, there must be...the risk of an impossibility" (*BG*, 561-2)? Here it looks like impossibility *dampens* desire, just as hope, in the case of the Duchesse, stokes it.

Do we really need jealousy, then, to keep things going? No, not that either. Swann continues to love Odette even after he's stopped being jealous: "once the desire to tear her away from every rival was no longer imposed by his jealousy upon his love, that love became once again, more than anything, a taste for the sensations which Odette's person gave him" (S, 432).

It's also not really true that our partner could be just about anybody, that her characteristics are totally immaterial, and that we essentially invent everything about her. Albertine, the narrator says, has soft hands, magnificent hair, and pretty cheeks. (He comes back to those cheeks many times.) She also has "great qualities of intelligence and heart" (C, 83). And these things matter to him.

In fact, it's a really important part of the Proustian picture of love that you find yourself subliminally attracted to a particular kind of person. As we saw in the case of Elstir and Gabrielle, your choice says something about you—indeed it comes from the deepest part of you. "If…Albertine might be said to echo something of the old original Gilberte, that is because a certain similarity exists, although the type evolves, between all the women we successively love, a similarity that is due to the fixity of our own temperament, which chooses them" (BG, 647). Albertine and Gilberte, the narrator explains elsewhere, and more wittily, "were women of a sort that would not attract the attention of men who for their part would go mad about other women who 'meant nothing' to me. A man has almost always the same way of catching cold, of falling ill; that is to say, he requires for it to happen a particular combination of circumstances; it is natural that when he falls in love he should love a certain type of woman" (F, 677).

So you don't just fall in love with someone because they're friends with a novelist, or because they're mean to you, or because an acquaintance sang their praises. You fall in love with them because, for better or worse, there's something in them that puts them in a particular category of people and something in you that draws you to that category of people, like butterflies to nectar or like moths to a flame. "I might have been able to feel that same exclusive love for another woman," says the narrator, "but not for any other woman" (*F*, 677). Love isn't nearly as random, delusional, or (necessarily) disastrous as it had seemed.

Five "first" moments

With all that in mind, let's come back to the question I asked you at the start of this chapter. When and why does Swann first fall in love with Odette? What's amazing, as Hervé Picherit shows, is that this "first" moment happens multiple times, and for multiple reasons. One scene that a lot of people talk about is the night Swann is unable to find Odette and drives around in increasing distress. That's what makes him fall in love with her, you might think, because "among all the modes by which love is brought into being...there are few so efficacious as this gust of feverish agitation that sweeps over us from time to time" (*S*, 326-7). But hold on...he already fell in love with her for the first time when she showed him affection, because, just as we saw with the Duchesse, "the feeling that [we] posse[ss] a woman's heart may be enough to make [us] fall in love with her" (*S*, 277). In fact the narrator says that Swann's hope—"that romantic hope, which alone had aroused and sustained his love, that a day might come when she would declare her passion" (*S*, 318-9)—is the *only* thing that made him fall in love, and even the only thing that made him *stay* in love. So Swann falls in love both because Odette is unavailable and because she's available! That's a bit odd.

And then there's the aesthetic dimension. Odette reminds Swann of a figure in a painting by Botticelli; that's another "first" reason for his affection. And a "little phrase" he hears in a sonata by Vinteuil prepares his heart for love ("those parts of Swann's soul in which the little phrase had obliterated all concern for material interests...were left vacant by it, blank pages on which he was at liberty to inscribe the name of Odette" (*S*, 336)). This is *after* the initial confidence and the anxious night; hasn't her name *already* been inscribed on his soul?

Oh, and Odette has also been recommended by Swann's friend Charlus, who says she's "ravishing." Having read the seventeenth-century philosopher La Rochefoucauld ("some people would never have fallen in love if they had never heard of love") and his own contemporary Gabriel Tarde, Proust was aware that imitation can sometimes be a force.

Between the recommendation, the music, the painting, the affection, and the anxiety, that's at least five different reasons for love. Why did Proust set things up this way? We'll come back to that toward the end of this book. For now, let's just say that the picture of love in the novel is complicated, and we shouldn't be tempted to take its narrator at face value. The main thing we can be sure of is that circumstances vary from one individual to another—each of us catches cold in our own way!—and it's precisely because circumstances vary that, as we'll see in the next chapter, love can be of such value in helping us understand ourselves.

The other thing we can say with certainty is that the narrator never finds what Elstir has found. His behavior in relationships, especially toward Albertine, can be highly troubling and at times frankly immoral; nor is love a source of stable happiness in his life. Love, for him, is *not* a way to forge meaningful connection with another human being, and *not* a route to enchantment. For "people like him," salvation has to come from somewhere else.

Same-sex relationships

Same-sex desire makes a substantial showing in Proust's novel, in a way that, while not totally unprecedented, is still pretty striking for the early decades of the twentieth century. Of course, it's one thing to mention a topic and another to treat it kindly, and André Gide complained that Proust had not done the latter. In his diary, Gide reports accusing Proust of wanting to "stigmatize uranism" (i.e. homosexuality) and grumbling that Proust never presented "this Eros in young and beautiful guise." Proust, according to Gide, admitted to having used all his happy memories of love in describing heterosexual encounters, leaving nothing but the "grotesque and abject" when it came to depicting characters like the Baron de Charlus.

Did Proust actually say that? Impossible to know. What we can know is that the first section of *Sodom and Gomorrah* had already been published, and that section, while it certainly makes Charlus seem ridiculous in some respects, also makes a glorious and entirely positive comparison: at the same moment when Charlus, a middle-aged aristocrat who prefers men in their twenties and thirties, meets Jupien, a youthful tailor who prefers older men, a bumblebee happens to fly into this urban courtyard, miles away from any countryside, and pollinates a flower. Both meetings, the narrator writes, are miracles.

This same section also includes a stunning lament for the plight of gay men (including poor Oscar Wilde, not named but clearly indicated), stretching across a monumental three-page sentence, the longest in the novel. Elsewhere, the Vinteuil septet—arguably the pinnacle of art within the *Search*, and the most important source of inspiration for the narrator—is made possible by the laborious rescue efforts of a lesbian (Mlle. Vinteuil's friend), staged by a gay man (Charlus), and performed by a bisexual violinist (Morel). Conversely, heterosexual love, as we just saw, is hardly presented as uniformly idyllic: Swann is miserable with Odette, Robert is miserable with Rachel, the narrator is miserable with Albertine, Albertine is miserable with the narrator.... So the reality is far from what Gide made it out to be.

What makes the situation complicated is the same thing that makes the issue of love in general complicated: the *Search* is a first-person novel, which means that we are seeing things through the eyes of a character. This character, unlike Proust, is straight. He has never experienced any same-sex desire himself, and though he has a moment of wondering whether he might have

Imitation isn't everything

When two people fall in love with each other, imitation can *sometimes* be a force. But is it *always*? On this point, sociologist Gabriel Tarde was a lot more insightful than certain later French theorists. Unlike those theorists (who shall remain unnamed), Tarde knew that we're not all mere sheep helplessly following other people's lead. And Proust admired him for recognizing that: in an unpublished manuscript, Proust praised Tarde for giving "an important role to individuals" in his thinking (*MC*, 143).

As if to illustrate the idea, Proust builds a beautiful pair of scenes into the *Search*. The narrator, who knows all the sacrifices Saint-Loup has made for his girlfriend Rachel, finally meets her—and can't believe that this very ordinary individual is the person in question. Saint-Loup, who knows all the sacrifices the narrator has made for his girlfriend Albertine, finally sees a photograph of her—and can't believe that this very ordinary individual is the person in question. Neither of them feels the slightest interest in the other's partner. In Proust as in real life, we rarely fall in love with people just because somebody else does.

hidden tendencies in that direction, that moment is very brief. He doesn't understand same-sex desire; frequently fails to recognize it (Charlus's overtures are baffling to him); can't imagine it; is terrified by it in its female form (the prospect of Albertine cheating with a woman is more troubling to him than the prospect of her cheating with a man); and is made dizzy, if not panicked, by its male form. That, I think, is why his theories on the subject are so spectacularly incoherent.

In making his incoherent statements, the narrator draws on a set of influential nineteenth-century approaches, including those of

Richard von Krafft-Ebing (homosexuality as perversion or vice), Bénédict Morel (homosexuality as hereditary disease), and Karl Heinrich Ulrichs (homosexuality as the natural outcome of individuals ending up in a wrongly gendered body). The narrator uses the word "vice" more than once, wonders whether homosexuality is a "mal héréditaire" in the Guermantes family, and consistently uses Arrigo Tamassia's term "inversion," rather than Krafft-Ebing's "homosexuality," because of his investment in the Ulrichs-style wrong-body idea.

The wrong-body idea is applied to both men and women: Charlus at one point looks like his sister, "so salient at that moment was the woman whom a mistake on the part of Nature had enshrined in the body of M. de Charlus," while conversely, it may be Albertine's "vice" that "produced in her that honest, frank manner, creating the illusion that one enjoyed with her the same loyal and unqualified comradeship as with a man." (Here of course I'm just reporting, not endorsing, what the narrator has to say.) The wrong-body idea also leads the narrator to a tragic picture of male homosexuality, according to which each gay man wants to be with a man, but since other gay men are, like them, women in men's bodies ("hommes-femmes"), they can never have what they want.

The first two hypotheses are mutually contradictory: if something is a "disease" it can't be a "vice," since the notion of vice implies choice. (You can't *blame* someone for having pneumonia.) And they aren't even the only theories the narrator somehow seems to believe all at once. Maybe same-sex love is just, well, love, "with slight discrepancies due to the identity of sex." Maybe it's something positively beautiful, like an orchid. Maybe it goes still further beyond that, producing a profound "intensification of the intellectual qualities." So the narrator condemns, pities, studies, appreciates, admires, and envies Charlus and company, by turns. We should be grateful, he says wittily, that the angels did such a terrible job of eradicating the inhabitants of Sodom.

As for the "hommes-femmes" theory of same-sex desire, it seems to clash with features of the plot. What should we make of someone like Robert de Saint-Loup, who has a shift in orientation? More to the point, what should we make of characters who are (happily) bisexual, like Odette and Albertine?

Ultimately, the narrator's theories of same-sex desire end up telling us much less about it than about him. With male same-sex desire he's all over the map; with female same-sex desire, as Ladenson says, he's so mystified that he doesn't even *try* to explain it.

But there's something else going on here, something we can read between the lines. In Proust's novel, same-sex desire is often compared to Jewishness, with the phrase *en être*—"to be one of us," "to be one of them"—frequently attached to both. Same-sex orientation and Jewishness are both oppressed identities; both allow, to some extent, for "passing" (it's possible to conceal one's origins or one's preferences); both are features that an individual can downplay (like Gilberte and Robert) or proudly lay claim to (like Swann and Charlus in their later years); and both, most importantly, form communities that transcend boundaries of class and nation. (Here I am drawing on Erin Carlston's analysis in her book *Double Agents*.)

When, in 1894, Alfred Dreyfus was falsely accused of feeding military secrets to the Germans, his Jewishness clearly played a part, because some religions are taken to establish connections across national lines, making it quite possible for someone to have more in common with a German Jew than with a French Catholic. Meanwhile, in the world of same-sex desire, "the prince...on leaving the duchess's party goes off to confer in private with the ruffian."

So the reflection on sexual orientation is a reflection not just on identity but also on community. The community of gay men is one that carries its share of suffering in a prejudiced age, but the novel arguably presents it as preferable, nonetheless, to nationalism and to high society. In this world people bond over an authentic part of who they are, not over something artificial like "noble blood" or "national identity," let alone a shared disdain of outsiders. And it's more capacious than friendship or even family. Perhaps, then, it hints at a better form of life in common, one only rivaled, in Proust, by a community of shared aesthetic appreciation.

A novel is not a treatise

We've just seen something really interesting about the depiction of love in Proust, whether same-sex or opposite-sex: it often goes against what the narrator says. The narrator's *theory* tells us that love objects are interchangeable, that you only fall in love because you fear the other person isn't interested, and that things between you remain forever precarious. But the novel's reality is that you can fall in love with someone who incarnates your ideal of beauty. Gabrielle is *not* interchangeable; Elstir was *not* attracted by her unavailability; and everything between them is *not* disastrous.

Even when the narrator's general statements aren't being contradicted by what we see in the plot, they often contradict each other. We saw that happening with the origins of love ("it's always about unavailability—no, availability can do it too!"), and also with same-sex desire, which sometimes looks like a "vice" (to be castigated), sometimes an "illness" (to be pitied), sometimes a "taste" (to be recognized), sometimes a blessing (to be envied). Here too, we need to resist taking any particular statement at face value.

A third reason to doubt the narrator's universal accuracy is that he periodically changes his mind about things. The first volume ends with a poignant statement about the transitory nature of experience. Beautiful! Powerful! And...bogus! Fascinatingly,

Proust told critic Jacques Rivière that the passage in question was "the *opposite* of my conclusion," that this real conclusion would be revealed in the final volume, and that his plan was "to depict errors, without feeling compelled to say that I consider them to be errors; too bad for me if the reader believes I take them for the truth." (Side-note: if you're in a class or reading group that only assigns volume 1, you may be getting shortchanged.)

At times the narrator will retract something almost immediately, as though eager to keep us on our toes. ("That is why the better part of our memories exists outside us.... Outside us? Within us, rather..." (*BG*, 300).) All of these moves are designed to remind us that we're reading a special kind of book. Since Proust wrote his novel in the first person, and often drew on events from his own experience, it's understandable that many have seen the statements about the past as forming an autobiography and the statements about philosophy as forming a treatise. When the narrator talks about his past, those folks assume, that's Proust telling you his life story; when the narrator talks about ideas, that's Proust telling you what he thinks. But as we saw early on, the *Search* is not an autobiography. And as we're seeing now, it's also not a treatise. To use literary jargon, the narrator of this novel is not entirely "reliable."

This goes along with something Proust says in "On Reading," the preface to his translation of Ruskin's *Sesame and Lilies*. In the ideal case, Proust writes here, the thoughts we find in books are not conclusions but just "incitements," catalysts for a reflection we pursue on our own. "So long as reading is for us the inciter," he adds, "whose magic keys open to our innermost selves the doors of abodes into which we would not have known how to penetrate, its role in our life is salutary." But if we start to think that truth is "deposited between the leaves of books like honey ready-made by others," and that we can passively absorb it from the shelf of a library, "reading becomes dangerous" (*ORR*, 118). Dangerous!

Love and sex

39

So when the narrator of *In Search of Lost Time* makes confident pronouncements about life, the universe, and everything, we shouldn't automatically trust them; we shouldn't automatically take them, that is, as being endorsed by Proust. (Pro tip: if you find yourself tempted to say things like "Proust ate a madeleine that brought back his childhood," or "Proust said homosexuality is a vice," try saying "Proust's narrator" instead. You'll always be safe.)

Even statements of fact shouldn't automatically be trusted. On one page the narrator says Albertine has a mole on her chin (*BG*, 578); forty pages later, he says he was wrong, since it's really on her cheek (*BG*, 618); six pages after that, he says it was on her upper lip the whole time (*BG*, 624-5). A wonderful example of "depict[ing] errors, without feeling compelled to say that I consider them to be errors."

All this said, it's really important not to go to the other extreme and reject every single claim the narrator makes. Some of them we know to be endorsed by Proust, since we have correspondence, essays, and an interview to draw on. That "interview" wasn't much of one—Proust probably wrote out his side of the text, rather than engaging in a Q&A—but it's pretty revealing nonetheless. Here Proust tells us that his work is dominated by the distinction between voluntary and involuntary memory, that each of us experiences the world differently, and that this difference emerges in aesthetic style. Likewise, the essay on Flaubert talks about "grammatical singularities" expressing a "new vision" (*EA*, 288); we find similar remarks in the article on Moreau and the preface to Paul Morand's *Tendres Stocks*; and as we saw in chapter 1, the preface to Jacques-Emile Blanche's *Propos de peintre* takes a swipe at Sainte-Beuve for "explaining the true Fantin or Manet, the one that is only found in their work, on the basis of the mortal man" (*EA*, 273-4).

So we end up with an interesting situation, in which some of the universal statements tell us about *life*, while others just tell us about the *narrator*. (As he says himself, in a rather ironic maxim, "our ideas have only a symptomatic value" (*F*, 757).) His chaotic assertions about homosexuality, remember, reveal merely that he's panicked by it.

And the very fact that he produces so many of these universal statements tells us something else: he loves generalizing! He loves it in part because it makes him feel better about things; he's no longer alone, and he's at least a little in control of his situation. (When, at one point, he's able to see his tormented love affair as just an example of a common predicament, this thought brings him "immense... relief" (*C*, 490).)

So what are we to do, as readers? How can we know if a given assertion is something Proust believes, something only the narrator believes, something *part* of the narrator believes, or something part of the narrator believes *temporarily*? Well, we can definitely trust ideas that also show up in Proust's nonfiction writings. For the rest, I recommend considering statements innocent until proven guilty—which is to say, taking them seriously unless they conflict with other claims made by the narrator (like the remarks about same-sex desire) or with events depicted in the book (like the remarks about love). It's tricky, but that's part of the point: this book wants us to work. We'll see later on why the effort pays off.

Chapter 5
Knowledge and ignorance

In chapter 2 we learned that Proust's narrator is in search of many things, none of them really being time. He's looking, above all, for enchantment and purpose; but he's also looking for connection with other people, connection with himself, and connection with the world. We've just seen how love fails to satisfy his desire for meaningful connection with another human being. We'll see in chapter 9 how his connection to himself begins to fray—how it begins to feel as though he's a totally different creature from the person who occupied his body ten years ago, or even ten minutes ago—and what he does to overcome that. But can't he at least have a simple connection with the world?

Knowing the world

No such luck. "In all perception there exists a barrier," the narrator writes, "as a result of which there is never absolute contact between reality and our intelligence" (*TR*, 420). That barrier is the "perspective" we encountered in chapter 3. By modifying everything that reaches us from the outside world, this perspective prevents us from ever accessing it directly.

It actually does that in two separate ways. First, every single one of us perceives the sun as rising in the morning, for example, when in reality it's the earth that's moving; that's the universal aspect of perspective. But only the narrator sees steeples as legendary maidens, and only I see scallops as the cilantro of the marine realm. That's the second aspect of perspective, the individual aspect, the one that makes my world different from your world. ("The universe," writes the narrator, "is true for all of us and different for each of us" (*C*, 250).) It causes some things to stand out as special and others to retreat into the background. It puts objects into idiosyncratic categories (salmon, yum! cilantro, yuck!). And above all, it endows them with a value that looks objective but that really comes from you.

It's this phenomenon the narrator has in mind when he says we "have the sensation of being always enveloped in, surrounded by our own soul…. We try to discover in things, which become precious to us on that account, the reflection of what our soul has projected on to them; we are disillusioned when we find that they are in reality devoid of the charm which they owed, in our minds, to the association of certain ideas" (*S*, 119).

In other words, it's our mind—in particular, the individual aspect of our perspective—that makes things in the world seem precious, by projecting its desires onto them. That, of course, is a recipe for endless disappointment, since people, places, and objects are almost never going to live up to our hopes for them; plus it means we feel forever cut off from the world around us, hearing only the echo of our own imaginings everywhere we turn. If that's where things stopped in Proust, they would be pretty bleak. But luckily it isn't.

Surprise

It might be tempting to imagine that each of us is trapped indefinitely in our own tiny bubble, cut off from an accurate understanding of anything. But that would be going too far: "in spite of whatever may stem from various subjective points of view, the fact remains that there is a certain objective reality" (*GW*, 780). How do we know objective reality exists? Answer: surprise.

When the narrator visits the seaside town Balbec, for example, his hotel room is like nothing he had imagined, and "there is perhaps nothing that gives us so strong an impression [as this] of the reality of the external world" (*BG*, 332). That new room is a surprise that's only mildly unpleasant, but surprises can also be searingly painful, like Albertine's jealousy-inducing revelation of her connection with Mlle Vinteuil ("something which my mind would never have been capable of inventing" (*SG*, 703)), or welcome, as when a beautiful face offers an "element which we are powerless to invent" (*BG*, 205). Either way, they show us that we are not just hallucinating the world, that it exceeds our capacity to dream it up.

So that's a pretty good start, by way of talking us down from the ledge of subjective idealism. But it gets even better. Not only can we know that there's an objective reality out there; we can also know what it is, a fair amount of the time. Yes, perspective distorts everything, like a funhouse mirror, but in many cases, the mind can set things straight—in the same way that, when you see a straw in a glass of water, you're fully aware it isn't bent.

That's what happens when the narrator eventually figures out where Albertine's mole is. (It doesn't keep moving around forever.) That's what happens, too, when he hears the ticking of Saint-Loup's watch, "from behind, from in front of me, from my right, from my left"; as soon as he finally lays eyes on it, "I heard the tick in a fixed place from which it did not move again" (*GW*, 92). And it's also what allows him to be certain that Charlus is into men, and that Mlle Vinteuil has had a same-sex encounter: "this time at least, I had no need to 'seem to know' . . . : I *knew*, I had *seen*" (*C*, 451).

Another way to put this, using Proustian language, is that the *intellect*, or rational mind, corrects the *intuition*, or instinctive mind. ("We should never succeed in identifying objects," says the narrator, "if we did not bring reasoning to bear on them"

44

(*GW*, 574).) It's true that the intuition frequently gets there first, seizing on reports from the senses and painting them in its own special colors. But the intellect, though a relative slowcoach—"intelligence…like the sound of thunder travels less rapidly" (*F*, 731)—can usually manage to straighten the bent straw in the end. Knowledge of the world turns out to be possible after all.

And because knowledge of facts is often possible, knowledge of more general *truths* is sometimes possible too. In areas where we're able to gather decent data, we can safely extrapolate from those to general principles. (Even when it comes to the realm of medicine, the narrator says, "from this mass of errors a few truths have in the long run emerged" (*GW*, 405).) One important consequence for us: some of the narrator's universal statements about memory, identity, and art may actually be reliable.

Still, we should be careful what we wish for: knowledge of the world is, for the most part, hardly enchanting. It reveals the drab reality of a town we've fantasized about, the ordinariness of an aristocrat, the deceitfulness of a partner, the non-magical nature of trees in a park.… Knowledge like this is not going to give the narrator what he most deeply wants. In fact, as we're about to see, errors about the world are sometimes going to do a better job—partly because illusions are indispensable, and partly because they lead us to truths about ourselves.

Knowing yourself

So let's think about how, in Proust, we discover those truths about ourselves. Just as with knowledge of the world, there are major roadblocks; you can easily be wrong about what you want and what you believe. That's what happens—delightfully—when the narrator, who has recently developed an interest in Albertine, is getting ready to go somewhere he knows he'll see her: an unconscious part of his mind knows that he wants this more than anything, but the conscious part foolishly thinks he doesn't care ("my brain assessed this pleasure at a very low value now that it was assured" (*BG*, 614-5)). Luckily the unconscious part takes control, making sure he gets there on time.

You're in even greater trouble when it comes to knowing your "true self," that perspective which tints everything with its magical colors. The problem here is that a perspective is something we look *through*, not *at*; it's a part of you that can never be seen, since it is always doing the seeing. Or as the narrator puts it, "throughout the whole course of one's life, one's egoism sees before it all the time the objects that are of concern to the self, but never takes in that 'I' itself which is perpetually observing them" (*F*, 628).

So how can you know what you think, why you act, and who you are? Well, for beliefs and desires the (ingenious) trick is to treat yourself as though you were somebody else: inspect your own behavior, then draw conclusions about what its cause must be, just as you would if you were trying to figure out what's going on with a friend. "The memory of Mme de Guermantes at the Opera," the narrator says at one point, "must have been charming...since it was always to it...that my ideas of love returned" (*GW*, 72-3). "Must have"? Normally we assume that the way to know what you're thinking is by looking inside yourself—philosophers call this "introspection"—but Proust's narrator clearly feels this isn't going to do him any good. He knows that his own mind is too crafty, too cloudy. The only way to outwit it is to imagine it belongs to a stranger.

As for your perspective, the trick here is what we saw when we discussed the steeples at Martinville. We know how things look to us when we first set eyes on them; we can also figure out how they are in reality. Well, subtract the one from the other and you get your own personal index of refraction, the odd way your mind—and your mind alone—rearranges and colors the world we all otherwise share.

Falling in love is a fantastic source of data here. (Personally, I think love is also good for other reasons, but Proust's narrator wouldn't always agree.) Remember what the narrator said about the way we pick our partners: "a certain similarity exists... between all the women we successively love, a similarity that is due to the fixity of our own temperament, which chooses them." So if you fall in love more than once, you can start to see a pattern.

This is the upside of the rather pessimistic view of romance we saw in chapter 4. "I had guessed long ago," the narrator reports, "that when we are in love with a woman we simply project on to her a state of our own soul"; as a consequence, "the emotions which a perfectly ordinary girl arouses in us can enable us to bring to the surface of our consciousness some of the innermost parts of our being" (*BG*, 563-4). If you're paying attention, in other words, you'll start to notice your "type" emerging, your lifelong ideals, the unchanging inner world that, for better or worse, makes you who you are.

So if you have a terrible track record with relationships, take comfort: you are the one to blame.

Knowing other people

With a bit of work, then, you can know facts about the world (by using your intellect to correct initial impressions), general truths about life (by extrapolating from those facts), information about yourself (by working back from your own actions, as though you were a stranger), and even a sense of your own perspective (by noticing who you fall in love with, how you speak and write and paint, and what comes to mind when you look at trees and steeples). But how much can you know about other people?

The short answer is: it depends. When it comes to their deepest identity, that's off the table. (Unless they happen to be artists;

more on that later.) This is a special kind of knowledge, one philosophers would call "knowledge by acquaintance." Here, you don't just want to know where they grew up, who their favorite poet is, or what they did on a given day: you want to know what it's like to be them. You want to imagine desiring what they desire, fearing what they fear, and connecting what they connect; to sense how things look when they see them, sound when they hear them, feel when they touch them.

In the narrator's case, one thing he desperately wants to know, when trying to project himself into Albertine's mind, is what it's like to be a woman who loves women. And he finds it impossible, since "this love between women was something too unfamiliar; there was nothing to enable me to form a precise and accurate idea of its pleasures, its quality" (*C*, 519). Of course, bisexuality doesn't *define* Albertine—she is plenty else besides her orientation, and she is not identical to every other bisexual woman in the novel (Odette, for example)—but it's nonetheless an important part of her essence, and a part the narrator will forever find inaccessible.

Even when it comes to simply knowing *facts* about other people, the situation is pretty dire. You can do fairly well as long as it's someone you aren't involved with—the narrator ultimately has no difficulty, for example, learning that Charlus is gay—"but as soon as we have a desire to know," other people become "a dizzy kaleidoscope in which we can no longer distinguish anything" (*F*, 699-700).

If, say, you suspect your partner of cheating, you obviously aren't going to trust that partner to tell you the truth. Nor should you trust your friends, some of whom will lie to protect you, others to hurt you. Worst of all, your own sleuthing may not work, since your reasoning powers are constantly being thrown out of kilter by your emotions. ("My desire," the narrator says, "by utilizing the powers of my intelligence . . . [,] had put me on the wrong track" (*F*, 824).)

48

That may be a fairly common idea—we all rationalize bad news, let motivated reasoning take over, explain things away—but the narrator adds a brilliant twist. It's not just desire that hijacks the mind, he says: it's also fear. "If my reason, in seeking to bring about my cure, let itself be guided by my desire, on the other hand…my instinct, in trying to make me ill, might have allowed itself to be led astray by my jealousy" (*C*, 495). Jealousy makes you too skeptical, just as love makes you too credulous.

You might think that intellect here is simply a chump, foolishly believing a pack of lies, and that intuition is a voice of truth gnawing away in the back of your head. But no, that's not the case. Intuition doesn't want to produce enlightenment; it wants to cause pain. Its mission being to "make [you] ill," it keeps feeding you suspicions, whether or not they're well founded. If intellect is a consolation machine, intuition is a torment machine, an instrument for telling you what you don't want to hear.

So even if you could bring yourself to trust the voice of doubt, that wouldn't necessarily get you closer to the facts. (We should not, the narrator warns, "end up with the mistake of regarding one supposition as more true than the rest simply because it [is] the most painful" (*SG*, 316).) About someone you love, all you can ever have is an antithetical pair of guesses: "we understand the characters of people to whom we are indifferent, but how can we ever grasp that of a person who is an intimate part of our existence,…whose motives provide us with an inexhaustible source of anxious hypotheses, continually revised?" (*BG*, 648)

There's only one thing left to do at this stage, and that's split the difference. "I tried," the narrator says at one point, "to discover between these two perspectives, equally distorting, a third which would enable me to see things as they really were" (*BG*, 221). And we often see him doing a little dialectic: try out one hypothesis (e.g. the Guermantes are supernatural), shift to a completely opposite hypothesis (e.g. the Guermantes are just like anyone else),

49

then end up somewhere in the middle (the Guermantes are actually quite witty).

This seems like a good strategy, right? If your intellect is always telling you what you most want to hear, and your intuition is always telling you what you least want to hear, mustn't the truth be halfway between the two? Not so fast. Albertine's behavior *could* be a mix of loyalty and betrayal, but she could also be totally fickle, or even completely faithful. Her section of the book ends with a sentence that simply gives up: "truth and life are very difficult to fathom, and I retained of them, without having really got to know them, an impression in which sadness was perhaps actually eclipsed by exhaustion" (*F*, 843). If you're genuinely in love, you'll never really know the person you're in love with. Especially if you're the jealous type.

And yet, and yet… what if everything I've said is untrue? What if knowledge of other people *is* possible in Proust, even when it's about their essence, and even when they're close to us? What if the narrator is just convincing himself to believe otherwise, because it's comforting to think his failure to understand Albertine is not his fault, and, reversely, that she cannot see the dysfunctional person that he really is? Some interpreters have made highly compelling arguments for reading it that way. Could the narrator be wrong here too, just as he so often is about love?

Knowing what not to know

Whatever you decide about that, the picture of knowledge in Proust remains rich and complicated. Can you get beyond the barrier of subjectivity and come to know things? That depends on whether you're talking about the world or about people. If you're talking about the world, you also have to specify whether you want knowledge of specific facts or knowledge of general laws. And if you're talking about people, you have to specify whether you want knowledge of yourself or of others; if others, whether strangers or lovers; if lovers, whether their beliefs and actions or the depths of their soul. Some things are fairly easy to sort out. Some take a lifetime. Some remain, perhaps, forever out of reach.

But is it always knowledge that we're looking for in the first place? Part of Proust's brilliance lies in recognizing that it's not, that sometimes illusions are far more valuable than the truths that would displace them—and that these illusions continue to function, and gain in dignity, when we recognize them for what they are.

To start with, while we can often get the facts about the world, and while they're often good to know, the mistakes we fall into can be just as important. After all, it's the errors we make—the idiosyncratic way we idealize a partner, the weird things we see in a steeple—that show us who we are. And it's who we are as individuals, and who others are as individuals, that can bring the world to life.

That comes out very clearly in the little prose poem we discussed in chapter 3, the one that's only superficially about a group of steeples. There's nothing particularly special or magical about those steeples; what makes them worth writing about are the waves they make in the narrator's head, the inner chain reactions they trigger. What we care about above all is the inner life, not the outer world; the phenomenology, not the reality.

Second, illusions can be valuable for their own sake, not just for what they have to teach us about our minds. Midway through volume 2, we find the narrator taking a train to seaside town Balbec. "The journey was one that would now no doubt be made by motor-car," he says, "with a view to making it more agreeable... [and] accomplished in such a way, it would even be in a sense more real, since one would be following more closely, in a more intimate contiguity, the various gradations by which the surface of the earth is diversified. But after all the specific

51

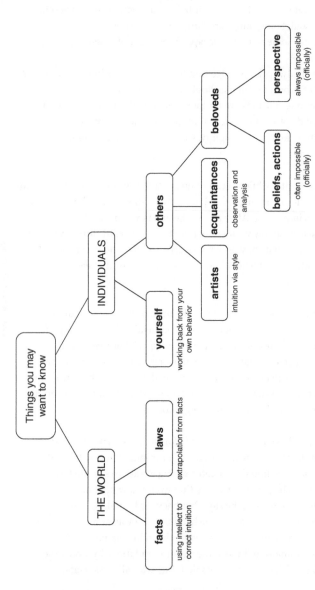

8. A tentative diagram summarizing what I take to be the official picture, in Proust, of what we can know and how.

attraction of a journey lies...in its making the difference between departure and arrival...as intense as possible" (*BG*, 301-2).

Train travel makes us feel, as strongly as possible, the difference between the place we started from and the place we're going. Car travel gives us more truth—it shows us that places are not magically unique, not radically distinct from everything around them—but train travel, by covering up the gradual transitions, gives us more enchantment; and sometimes enchantment is the thing that matters.

And some illusions, third, aren't just enchanting but positively essential for our mental health. Does it really help to recognize that one day the sun will cool and all human life will be extinguished? Or, as the narrator adds, that the remaining animals won't read any of our books (*C*, 240)? "Truth," says the narrator, "is not always compatible...with life" (*TR*, 314); for knowledge like that, maybe the best thing we can learn is how to forget.

So clear-eyed awareness can often be wonderful—not to mention vital for our survival—but we'd better also be able to forget, and embellish, and plug our ears, and take the train from time to time. And the amazing thing is that the forgetting, embellishing, ear-plugging, and train-taking continue to function even when we do them consciously.

When the narrator decides that his love for Gilberte is not reciprocated, he sets about mending his broken heart, gradually convincing it to relinquish its strong feelings for her. To do that, he needs to stay away from her; and to do that, he needs to keep declining the invitations she sends him. But how can you bring yourself to spurn opportunity after opportunity to see the person you care most about in the world? Answer: by pretending it isn't forever. "I said to myself: 'This is the last time that I shall refuse an invitation to meet her; I shall accept the next one.' To make our separation less difficult to realize, I did not picture it to myself as final. But I knew very well that it would be" (*BG*, 251).

This is a fascinating example, showing that illusions in Proust can be not just *necessary* (he needs the trick in order to keep declining the invitations; he needs to keep declining in order to cure himself) but also *lucid* (he "knows very well" that he'll continue his pretense until Gilberte stops inviting him) and indeed *deliberate* (he feeds himself lies intentionally). Even when you're fully aware of the ruse you're pulling on yourself, it works. Proust's novel is as much about (deliberate) illusion as it is about truth— and truth, surprising as it may sound, does not always come out on top.

Chapter 6
Inclusion and exclusion

For a book that's mostly about memory, selfhood, art, and love, a remarkable amount of time is spent in salons. We're invited to gatherings hosted by the inane Verdurins, an overreaching middle-class couple who want to look like aristocrats; by the Duchesse de Guermantes, an actual aristocrat; and by the highly sought-after Princesse de Guermantes, an even fancier aristocrat. And none of these circles offers much to write home about.

Time wasted: The social world

To be fair, not *everyone* we meet in salons is entirely vapid, conceited, small-minded, and callous. The Princesse de Parme has true kindness (something of a rarity around here). The Duchesse de Guermantes isn't a creature from another world, as the narrator had hoped—indeed she can be stunningly heartless, as when she pretends a friend isn't dying just so she can get to a party—but she has an intelligence and wit that set her apart from most of her high-class friends. Swann and Charlus know and appreciate the arts. Robert de Saint-Loup favors the life of the mind over the petty vanities of his set. Cottard, the "imbecile," is also a talented doctor. And "Biche," the ridiculous painter, will later turn out to be the great Elstir. Still, for the most part the endless chit-chat is a colossal waste of time, *temps perdu* in the bleakest sense.

In fact it's worse than that: high society is almost a negative image of everything the narrator desires. Where he craves access to the deep truth of other people, society is all about being as fake as possible. Where he yearns for passionate commitment and genuine connection, society offers ironic detachment. Where he seeks secular re-enchantment, Verdurin life looks like a perverse facsimile of the worst aspects of religion, from excessively "faithful" acolytes to excommunications. The narrator wants depth, but finds superficiality; wants mystery, but finds banality; wants variety, but finds conformity. And one thing he loves in art is its *generosity*, its capacity to help us out in the many ways we'll see in the next chapter; salons, by contrast, are full of back-stabbing selfishness and Machiavellian social climbing. (The power hunger, spite, and vindictiveness of the Verdurins are a sight to see.)

What do these pointless, soulless encounters do for the people who attend them? One possibility is that they offer a sense of belonging, together with a collective type of identity. (Here and in what follows, I am drawing on a wonderful chapter by Edward Hughes.) While he's with the Verdurins, Cottard can tell himself he's part of something, included, welcome; he can also tell himself that he is a *fidèle*, a member of the sect, "one of us." In such cases, though, inclusion for some always depends on exclusion for others. (To feel special—to feel like an insider—you have to know that many can't have it, don't get it, aren't in the loop.) It's only because someone else is "out" that Cottard is "in." Indeed it's only because someone else is out that there's such a thing as being "in" at all.

As Hughes has pointed out, we see the same structure replicated up and down the Proustian social world, from upper-class Guermantes through high-bourgeois Verdurins to Aunt Léonie and the generally beloved housekeeper Françoise, who viciously torments the poor kitchen maid. And we see it replicated at every scale, from households all the way to nations. The majority heterosexual state disdains, ostracizes, and even punishes those who seek the company of their own sex. (The trials of Oscar Wilde and of Prince Philipp von Eulenburg are still very recent.) The majority Christian state also disdains those born Jewish. (The Dreyfus affair, in which a Jewish captain was wrongly convicted of transmitting military secrets to the Germans, imprisoned, freed, retried, re-imprisoned, and finally exonerated, stretched from 1894 to 1906; Proust was a vocal "Dreyfusard.") The French-speaking state, relatedly, comes to despise everything German—even operas, poems, and philosophy—as the two nations gradually inch closer to war.

Each of these is a system of inclusion and exclusion: you're either "one of us" or "one of them." Each has gatekeepers making it difficult for an outsider to come in, while also standing ready to kick unworthy insiders out. And each has principles of inclusion

9. Salons, in Proust's novel, are a venue for life-changing musical performances...but otherwise a colossal waste of time.

and exclusion that seem highly *arbitrary*. Is someone born in France, or attracted to people of a different gender, or of Christian ancestry, really better than someone born in Germany, or attracted to people of the same gender, or of Jewish heritage? Is anything more than tribal loyalty—"ours good, theirs bad"—really driving such practices? To paraphrase Hughes again, it's as though there's a pleasure to be had simply in belonging, and as though belonging, tragically, always requires showing others the door.

Social mobility

And yet... for all the fierceness of the gatekeepers, it's not entirely impossible to placate them. The good townsfolk in Combray are gently mocked for thinking that no one ever changes status, that everyone lives from birth to death in exactly the same social spot. In reality, middle-class individuals constantly jockey for prestige. And high society, surprisingly, is permeable too: Swann, who is Jewish, is already well established there by the time the novel starts. Something more amazing still happens much later in the novel, but since it's one of the great surprises, I won't spoil it. I'll just say that you can find it on page 387 of *Time Regained*.

There can even be wholesale upheavals within high society, as when the Dreyfus affair unleashes a wave of antisemitism, and suddenly Jews like Swann are "out." "Like a kaleidoscope which is every now and then given a turn," the narrator explains, "society arranges successively in different orders elements which one would have supposed immutable, and composes a new pattern" (*BG*, 122).

By the end of the novel, that kaleidoscope appears to start turning with a newly dizzying force. Central aristocratic characters have fallen in status; central middle-class characters, by contrast, have arrived. Are we witnessing the decline of the aristocracy *as a class*, displaced by the rising bourgeoisie? Is it the end of an era? And is an even more radical shake-up about to take place?

Perhaps symbolically, Combray—last survivor of the premodern attitude toward social change—is severely damaged in the War, its church destroyed. Meanwhile, the Russian Revolution breaks out in 1917, and the novel seems to wonder, in a sly wink, whether something similar could happen in France. While the rich diners sit down to their meal at the Balbec hotel, the working population collects outside the windows to observe them, as though looking at tropical fish in an aquarium; and it's "an important social question," the narrator comments, "whether the glass wall will always protect the banquets of these weird and wonderful marvelous creatures, or whether the obscure folk who watch them hungrily out of the night will not break in some day to gather them from their aquarium and devour them" (*BG*, 354). For haves and have-nots alike, a very different future could be just around the corner.

A different kind of community

So the groups we see most prominently in Proust are not quite as closed or rigid as they may seem. But whether closed or open, they are a consistently destructive force. While they contain one or two good people, they don't exactly bring out the best in them; while they sometimes put culture on display, they rarely inspire it. They operate unjustly, breed conformity, and cramp the soul, drawing it away from itself. Is it possible to do any better?

One answer might be simply: no. Just stay at home, make your art (like Elstir in later life), cultivate your garden; society is inherently corrupting. But we saw earlier that the world of same-sex desire looks like a step up from nationalism, snobbery, and religious sectarianism. It's a world that's tragically subject to vicious social prejudice, and a world with its own internal tensions, but it's one whose members bond, courageously, over an authentic part of who they are.

And maybe the virtual community of aesthetic appreciators is a similar gesture in the direction of utopia. (That's not, of course, to say that the two communities are mutually exclusive; Charlus, for example, belongs to both.) It's the narrator joining Bergotte in admiring Vermeer, Swann in loving Vinteuil. It's the audience at a performance relishing, together, the beauty of Racine and the brilliance of the actress's interpretation. (Very different from what we see at Mme Verdurin's salon, where many guests are distracted, gossiping, or striking a pose during the greatest musical performance of their lives.) It's the imaginary conversation we can have, across the miles and centuries, with the *Odyssey*, the *1001 Nights*, *Middlemarch*, or *Lohengrin*—even when, as in the last case, "our" country is at war with "theirs."

When it comes to a particular artwork or author, of course, there are still going to be insiders and outsiders. Some will enjoy Racine and others not; even the narrator's own future book will, he admits, not be helpful for everyone. But that doesn't mean a given person is barred from *all* aesthetic worlds. If you hate Racine, maybe you'll love Shakespeare. (To update the example, if you hate Murakami, maybe you'll love Morrison.) Each of us is an insider somewhere.

More importantly, outsiders here are those who *opt out*, rather than those who are unfairly kept at the door. Vinteuil's admirers— Swann, the narrator, Charlus, Mlle Vinteuil's friend— include people who are gay and straight, old and young, male and female, Jewish and Christian. Swann may find himself ostracized from many social circles (after Dreyfus), but nobody can stop him from loving the sonata. In this special kind of community, all are welcome, and no one is excluded because of who they are. No one is denied access on the grounds of race, class, nation, gender, or orientation; as long as society offers everyone an equal opportunity to enter these aesthetic worlds, it isn't anybody's fault if there's a lack of fit. So...could the virtual community of Proust fans itself be a kind of utopia? People like you and me? Lovers of Proust unite; you have nothing to lose but your pastries.

Chapter 7
Art and artists

Early on in this book, we saw that Proust's narrator is in search of all kinds of things that aren't time. He craves a meaningful purpose in life, a sense of identity, a measure of connection, a degree of belonging, and—his strongest need—a return to enchantment. High society, travel, and friendship don't do much of anything. Instances of involuntary memory do at least indicate the existence of a true self within him, something that resists the storms of change; and love choices and "impressions" provide a window onto its nature; but most of the narrator's deepest desires continue to go unsatisfied.

Periodically, however, the narrator reads a novel by Bergotte, looks at a painting by Elstir, or listens to a composition by Vinteuil. And what we see emerging from his thoughts about these canvases, compositions, and fictions—as well as his own, finally begun at the end of the last volume, *Time Regained*—is what he's been searching for all along. Art isn't just a better community; it's also a point of contact, an inspiration to self-fashioning, and a magic ticket to a secret kingdom.

The world

What kinds of contribution can artworks make to our lives? Let's start from the most familiar thought, which is that when it comes to novels, part of their value lies in the ideas they contain. This is clear from the *Search* itself, of course, and also from the way the narrator talks about Bergotte: "I longed to have some opinion...of his," he says, "upon everything in the world." (*S*, 134).

What's fascinating here, though, is that he soon decides Bergotte's opinions aren't actually true—the metaphysicians he comes to love in school "resemble him in nothing" (*S*, 134)—and yet he continues to admire his writing. So clearly ideas aren't *everything* when it comes to art. In fact, as we saw in chapter 4, Proust thinks novels shouldn't try to be treatises. It's fine for a work of fiction to be a hybrid, combining philosophical ideas and arguments with strictly aesthetic effects; but it cannot afford to be thoroughly preachy, prescriptive, didactic.

My world

This helps us to understand something slightly enigmatic that the narrator says about his own future book: it's not going to be (entirely) a mirror on the world but (also) a mirror for its readers, allowing them to be "the readers of their own selves" (*TR*, 508). Indeed when it comes to *any* good novel, "the writer's work is merely a kind of optical instrument which he offers to the reader to enable him to discern what, without this book, he would perhaps never have perceived in himself" (*TR*, 322). Rather than telling me the objective truth about something, a good novel helps me find out what *I* think about it. It gives me access to *my* world, rather than access to *the* world. It teaches me about me. It teaches you about you.

Why would we need a novel to do this for us? Well, remember what we saw earlier about self-knowledge: we are often wrong about our own minds. There are some questions we've never asked ourselves, and there are other issues we'd lie to ourselves about; introspection alone isn't going to do much good. So as with everything else, we need a detour—and one of the best detours, Proust's narrator thinks, is a great work of art.

Our world

Late in the second volume, the narrator is invited to Elstir's studio, where two canvases particularly attract his attention. One is a portrait of Odette in drag, from her younger days; the other is a landscape/seascape set in Carquethuit, a town near Balbec. Between them they indicate the third and fourth benefits of art.

The Carquethuit painting deliberately confuses land and sea. Masts look like steeples. Sand looks like waves. One part of the ocean looks like "a white stone causeway or ... a field of snow" (*BG*, 569). Elstir's plan, the narrator explains, is to present objects the way they appear to us, rather than the way they are in reality; it is "to reproduce things not as [Elstir] knew them to be but according to the optical illusions of which our first sight of them is composed" (*BG*, 570). (In one of his articles, Proust quotes J. M. W. Turner saying something similar: "my business is to draw what I see, and not what I know is there" (*ORR*, 42).)

As we saw in chapter 5, intellect eventually arrives to sort things into neat categories, but until that happens, perception is more confused; "surfaces and volumes are in reality independent of the names of objects which our memory imposes on them after we have recognized them" (*GW*, 574). We know, rationally, that the sea is water—but sometimes, for a few uncertain and delightful moments, it looks like a road. Art, here, is delivering "*our* world," the way in which life appears, whether rightly or wrongly, to the average human being. It gives us what philosophers would call "phenomenological data": information about how things *seem*, rather than how they actually are.

Her world

The other painting is different. It's a picture of Odette, and it resembles her somewhat, but it's not a faithful likeness, and it's also not just capturing optical illusions (for example, the way a person's hair color affects how we perceive her eyes). Here, what we're getting is the artist's individual *vision*. Elstir has dismantled the face of Odette and recomposed it in his own fashion, "substituting for it a rearrangement of the woman's features such as will satisfy a certain pictorial ideal of femininity which he carries in his head" (*BG*, 602). The portrait of Odette ends up looking like the portraits of other people Elstir has painted, because what they render is as much his general style as it is their specific traits. "Whatever the subject matter may be," the narrator says in a different context, an artist's style "remains identical with itself" (*C*, 343).

So we're finding again, in art, the two facets of perspective we met at the start of chapter 5. Optical illusions stand for the kind of mistake *everyone*'s brain makes, like perceiving the sun as "rising" in the morning. An artist's vision, by contrast, is an expression of the things *her* brain does, uniquely but consistently, to everything she sees and hears. Vision, for Vinteuil, is the "way in which he 'heard' the universe" (*C*, 505); it is the specific way the world feels to *him*, the "qualitative essence of [his] sensations" (*C*, 206).

It's worth stressing both of the adverbs I used in the last paragraph, "consistently" and "uniquely." An artist's vision reliably selects and arranges and colors things in the same way; and that way is not quite the same as anyone else's. (Thus Vinteuil's "song" is not just "different from those of other singers" but also "similar to all his own" (*C*, 342).) That, I think, is why the narrator often speaks of artists as having a "world."

Bergotte the writer has a world, "an unknown world towards which I was striving to raise myself" (*S*, 131). Elstir the painter and Vinteuil the composer have worlds too: "just as there was a certain world, perceptible to us in those fragments scattered here and there, in private houses, in public galleries, which was Elstir's world, the world he saw, the world in which he lived, so too the music of Vinteuil extended, note by note, stroke by stroke, the unknown, incalculable colorings of an unsuspected world" (*C*, 339-40). Even Johannes Vermeer, the real-life artist, paints canvases which are "fragments of an identical world" (*C*, 508).

This metaphor makes sense if you think about planets. Mars, for example, has a surface gravity of 3.71 m/s^2, about two and a half times less than Earth's; a year on Mars is 687 days, almost twice as long as ours. And everywhere you go on Mars, that surface gravity is the same. A world is something that has its own laws, laws that make it both individual and consistent—and artists are "worlds" in precisely that respect. As Proust puts it in an unpublished article on Gustave Moreau, "if a bird follows that poet" in a Moreau painting, "it is by virtue of other laws than those of our world" (*MPAL*, 348).

This "world"—this perspective—is of course the artist's "true self." (Art, says the narrator, is "a more profound reality, in which our true personality finds ... expression" (*C*, 204).) And that true self, as we saw in chapter 1, is completely different from the mask we wear when out in society. No one could ever have guessed, from the Vinteuil they encountered at Combray, what he contained within him: "this Vinteuil, whom I had known so timid and sad, had been capable—when he had to choose a timbre and to blend another with it—of an audacity, and in the full sense of the word a felicity, as to which the hearing of any of his works left one in no doubt" (*C*, 338). And no one could ever have suspected, if they had only known Elstir the individual, "that great painter's peculiar vision, which his speech in no way expressed" (*GW*, 574). Sainte-Beuve was 34 million miles from the truth.

"That ineffable something"

Proust's narrator sometimes draws a strong conclusion from this: the art you make is the *only* thing that can allow other people to see who you really are. Maybe it's even the only thing that can allow *you* to see who you are. "It alone," he says, "expresses for others *and renders visible to ourselves* that life of ours which cannot effectually observe itself" (*TR*, 300). No matter how close you are to someone else, how honest you try to be, or how many years you spend together, you'll never truly know each other. Your inner life is something that "cannot be transmitted in talk, even from friend to friend, from master to disciple, from lover to mistress" (*C*, 343); but "the harmony of a Wagner, the color of an Elstir, enable us to know that essential quality of another person's sensations into which love for another person does not allow us to penetrate" (*C*, 206).

That's partly, as we just saw, because we're never fully ourselves in society. But it's also because of the way language works: "that ineffable something which differentiates qualitatively what each of us has felt," the narrator suggests, is something each of us is "obliged to leave behind at the threshold of the phrases in which he can communicate with others only by limiting himself to externals, common to all and of no interest" (*C*, 343).

What's the narrator saying here? One way to think about it is that everyday language is common property, designed to solve coordination problems. Let's say there's a buffalo out there, and our little clan wants to figure out a strategy to trap it. Well, we're going to need our words to point to the same objects. The word "buffalo" needs to mean what a buffalo is to all of us, not what a buffalo is specifically to *me*. It doesn't matter if I was frightened by a buffalo when I was three, or you come from Buffalo, New York, or she dreams of being a buffalo in her next life—the core meaning of the word mustn't contain any of that. It has to be a lowest common denominator, the point on the Venn diagram where all our "buffalo" circles converge.

So conversation deals only with the impersonal; if you want to convey something personal, you need a special kind of language, one where what's being transmitted comes through not in the words themselves but in their organization. Literary language, like art more generally, hints at mental contents that live between the lines.

In other words, what expresses your unique perspective is not the *content* of your artwork—it's the *style*. As Proust stated in the 1913 interview, "style is in no way an embellishment, as certain people think; it is not even a question of technique; it is, like color with certain painters, a quality of vision, a revelation of a private universe which each one of us sees and which is not seen by others. The pleasure an artist gives us is that of discovering a whole new world" (*EA*, 255). "That's the miracle of literature," Simone de Beauvoir would later agree: "another person's thoughts become mine."

If you don't quite buy the strong version of this idea—art being the only thing allowing us to convey the essence of who we are, even to ourselves—perhaps you'll accept the milder version that seems to pop up here and there. "What interested me was not what they were trying to say but the manner in which they said it," the narrator tells us at one point, "and the way in which this manner revealed their character" (*TR*, 39); "our intonations," he adds elsewhere, contain "our philosophy of life" (*BG*, 667).

So maybe we don't need to compose symphonies or paint landscapes; maybe our vision of the world leaks out in everyday interactions. Perhaps we can express our true self in conversation, as long as we imbue it with a personal style. Still, the more effort we make to find an outlet for our perspective—to "sing in harmony with [our] native land" (*C*, 342-3), to engage in activities where we can be fully ourselves—the more chance there is that the miracle of communication will take place.

Flying from star to star

My experience with Proust is a bit unusual. When I was an undergraduate, I was supposed to read the whole of *Swann's Way*—more than 400 dense pages—in a week, gulp down some secondary criticism in a second week, and transmute it all, in a frenzied day, into an essay for my tutor. (Are you doing that right now? If so, I salute you.) After seven days I'd made it as far as page 72 and had forgotten everything I'd read. So I started over, and after a fortnight I made it back to page 72, at which point I had forgotten everything I'd read again, *and* run out of days in which to finish the volume, let alone write an essay. I panicked. It was the first and only time I skipped an assignment; I was terrified the university would send me packing. Thank you, Alison Finch, for being so kind to me.

Aside from terror, then, Proust didn't make much of an impression on me. If anything I sympathized with his first reviewer, Jacques Normand, who told publishing house Fasquelle that "reading cannot be sustained for more than five or six pages" and that "after infinite amounts of misery at being drowned in a sea of inscrutable developments and infinite amounts of maddening impatience at never returning to the surface—one has no notion, none, of what it's all about. What is the point of all this? What does all this mean? Where is all this going?"

I didn't think about Proust for many years (which, now I think about it, is itself very Proustian). But then one day the friend of a friend showed me this amazing pair of quotations, which she'd copied down in her notebook in the days before the internet. (You'll recognize parts of the first from earlier chapters, but the second may be new to you, just as it was to me.)

> 1. Style for the writer, no less than color for the painter, is a question not of technique but of vision: it is the revelation, which by direct

and conscious methods would be impossible, of the qualitative difference, the uniqueness of the fashion in which the world appears to each one of us, a difference which, if there were no art, would remain forever the secret of every individual. Through art alone are we able to emerge from ourselves, to know what another person sees of a universe which is not the same as our own and of which, without art, the landscapes would remain as unknown to us as those that may exist on the moon. Thanks to art, instead of seeing one world only, our own, we see that world multiply itself and we have at our disposal as many worlds as there are original artists, worlds more different one from the other than those which revolve in infinite space. (*TR*, 299)

2. A pair of wings, a different respiratory system, which enabled us to travel through space, would in no way help us, for if we visited Mars or Venus while keeping the same senses, they would clothe everything we could see in the same aspect as the things of Earth. The only true voyage, the only bath in the Fountain of Youth, would be not to visit strange lands but to possess other eyes, to see the universe through the eyes of another, of a hundred others, to see the hundred universes that each of them sees, that each of them is; and this we can do with an Elstir, with a Vinteuil; with people like these we do really fly from star to star. (*C*, 343)

Those passages are what made me fall in love with Proust. (Honestly; this is not a Swann and Odette situation, where I keep falling in love with Proust for the first time.) What a promise they make! It's an answer to the question the narrator has been asking all book long: how to escape from the world of the senses, how to transcend what we can see, hear, touch, and taste, how to find something beyond, something mysterious, something special and secret and valuable—but also something accessible. A world complete with its own laws. A world we can actually visit.

Most of us will never get to land on another planet; there's not much chance, either, that friendly aliens will venture out our way any time soon. We are, in a cosmic sense, alone, trapped down

10. Proust's manuscript page of the "style for the writer" sentence. Proust was endlessly adding to his text, jamming words inside sentences, sentences inside paragraphs; everything constantly grew from the middle.

here in our cage of isolation. And yet if Proust's narrator is right, then all of a sudden there are *multiple* Earths, as many as there are individual human beings. ("It is not one universe, but millions, almost as many as the number of human eyes and brains in existence, that awake every morning" (*C*, 250).) Each one of us sees the world a little bit differently, which means that each one of us sees a different planet Earth; and if we can *express* that difference in vision, by becoming artists, then we are multiplying the number of worlds that exist for everyone else. Strolling down a museum gallery is like coasting across space, flying from star to star.

With ordinary travel, famously, the problem is that we always bring ourselves. (Seneca put it nicely: "How can you wonder your travels do you no good, when you carry yourself around with you? You are saddled with the very thing that drove you away.") Even if we actually went to a populated planet, we would tend to reduce the unknown to the known, funneling everything via our existing categories. But what if we could see it through the eyes of the locals? That's what art does for us, without us even having to leave our armchair.

Proust's narrator isn't much of a religious person. And though he flirts periodically with supernatural possibilities—past lives, reincarnation, immortality, souls locked in trees, Platonic Forms, the unreality of the visible world—it's very unlikely he actually believes any of them. Where he finds enchantment is here on earth, in a this-worldly, fully secular expansion of experience. Christianity gave us transcendence in the form of God; art gives it to us in the form of paintings and symphonies, since entering a perspective is like teleporting to a different planet. Christianity set our finite lives inside something comfortingly infinite; art does the same. (As Friedrich Nietzsche put it, "the world has become 'infinite' for us all over again, inasmuch as we cannot reject the possibility that it may include infinite interpretations.") Christianity offered us mystery and wonder; art gives us jaw-droppingly perfect creations emerging from previously unimaginable ways of seeing. Christianity lent hidden depths to the world; art taps into a hidden depth within the soul. In spite of everything, the universe is enchanted anew.

The world transfigured

According to this picture of art—the "her world" picture, the one where what we're mainly getting is the artist's idiosyncratic perspective—the vision of the world is the thing that counts. And one consequence is that the subject matter can be more or less anything you like. "Everything is equally precious; the commonplace dress and the sail that is beautiful in itself are two mirrors reflecting the same image; their value is all in the painter's eye" (*GW*, 576).

Proust said something very similar in his own name, in a wonderful unfinished essay on painters Chardin and Rembrandt: "Chardin has taught us that a pear is as living as a woman, a kitchen crock as beautiful as an emerald. He has proclaimed the divine equality of all things under the light which beautifies them... objects in themselves are nothing" (*MPAL*, 334).

Art takes objects that start out banal, uninteresting, or even ugly—like scraps of food on a plate after dinner—and magically transfigures them into things of beauty. This is how it helps us feel at home in the world. And this is why it's "idolatry," as we saw, to make pilgrimages to places (including, ahem, "Illiers-Combray") that feature in works of art. It's a "superstition," says the narrator, that wrongly makes you think "they are superior to all things else, as if there dwelt in them already a great part of the work of art which they might be said to carry within them ready-made" (*BG*, 589). There's nothing special about Delft or Carquethuit; their value is all in the painter's eye.

Another interesting consequence of the expression view is that there is an *ethics of art*: if you *can* make something great, then you *should*, because you'll be doing the rest of the world a huge favor. Getting to grips with your self in this way isn't just narcissism; it is, in the narrator's brilliant phrase, an "egoism usable by others"

(*TR*, 513). It's OK to lock yourself away with your paint-brushes. It's OK not to accept invitations to parties, and even not to reply. The duty to make your work takes precedence, says the narrator, "over that of being polite" (*TR*, 435). (If you're writing the great American novel right now, don't bother answering your emails.)

And when you do put pen to paper or brush to canvas, you have an obligation to make sure you stay true to your vision. If you sell out, trying to please the public, you'll no longer be "sing[ing] in harmony with [your] native land," that inner world inside. Paradoxically, it's possible to fail to be yourself; it takes a lot of effort to be who you are. Your task, in a sense, is to get out of your own way, allowing your true self to shine through your work. Only by being yourself can you make the world brighter for everyone else.

Art as formal model

So far we've looked at four different things that artworks can do for us. They can show us *the* world, *our* world, *her* world, or *my* world: that is, they can reveal something about reality, about the human experience of it, about the artist, or about the individual spectator. But there is also a benefit Proust's narrator doesn't mention explicitly, and it turns out to be one of the most important.

Late in the fifth volume, the narrator goes to a society soirée where he hears Vinteuil's masterpiece, a septet. The septet is magnificent in itself, and he fully appreciates it for what it has to offer on its own terms (including the access it gives to Vinteuil's mysterious inner world). At the same time, though, he notices traces within it of Vinteuil's earlier work. And a fascinating thought suddenly strikes him:

> I began to realize that if, in the body of this septet, different elements presented themselves one after another to combine at

the close, so also Vinteuil's sonata, and, as I later discovered, his other works as well, had been no more than timid essays, exquisite but very slight, beside the triumphal and consummate masterpiece now being revealed to me. And I could not help recalling by comparison that, in the same way too, I had thought of the other worlds that Vinteuil had created as being self-enclosed as each of my loves had been; whereas in reality I was obliged to admit that just as, within the context of the last of these—my love for Albertine—my first faint stirrings of love for her (at Balbec at the very beginning, then after the game of ferret, then on the night when she slept at the hotel, then in Paris on the foggy Sunday, then on the night of the Guermantes party, then at Balbec again, and finally in Paris where my life was now closely linked to hers) had been, so, if I now considered not my love for Albertine but my whole life, my other loves too had been no more than slight and timid essays that were paving the way, appeals that were unconsciously clamoring, for this vaster love: my love for Albertine. (*C*, 335-6)

What's happening here is that the narrator is borrowing the structure of the septet as a way of thinking about his life with Albertine. Before, that relationship was just a disjointed series of events: meeting Albertine, flirting with her, getting rebuffed, finally kissing on a later meeting, drifting apart, coming back together, moving in. But now it's a *story*—a story of love, however tormented, overcoming obstacles and growing into the core of his existence. It has a single overarching *shape*, a single cadence, a single emotional tone.

And there's more: this story fits into a *bigger* story, the story of his romantic life in general. The Gilberte episode and the Albertine episode belong together, as part of a larger structure; they produce something that's more than the sum of its parts, just as a piece of music produces something more than the sum of its notes, motifs, or movements.

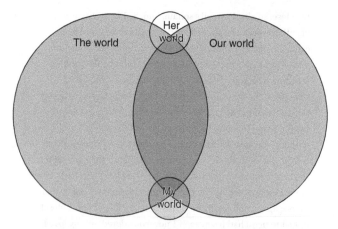

11. Artworks can provide insight into reality ("the world"), into the way things appear to human beings ("our world"), into the way things appear to the writer ("her world"), and even into the way things appear to the reader ("my world").

So the music serves, for our narrator, as a "formal model." It's a template, a blueprint, a mold to pour his own memories into. Or to change the analogy, it's like a dress pattern: you bring the material, but the pattern tells you where to cut it, where to seam it, how to sew it together.

Paving the way

There's one last thing to notice here. "My other loves," the narrator says, had been "paving the way" for the relationship with Albertine, the big love in his life. That's an interesting choice of term, suggesting something less like causation and more like foreshadowing.

When we think about story form, we tend to focus on cases where one thing leads to another, and that other to the next, in a perfect causal chain. ("Emma Bovary reads too many bad books,

76

and *therefore* gets the wrong idea about love, which *leads* her to make some poor life choices.") But causation isn't the only way two events can be linked. The adolescent flirtation with Gilberte didn't *make* our narrator fall in love with Albertine, or even make him fall in love in this particular way. Instead the two relationships send out echoes to each other across the long novel, just like a motif that returns in a symphony. The Gilberte episode foreshadows the Albertine episode, as a soothsayer's prophecy in Act 1 foreshadows—but doesn't cause—an outcome in Act 5. Once we get to the Albertine chapter, the memory of Gilberte lingers around to imbue the situation with richness, layering, and depth. "When new moments of pleasure call to us," the narrator writes, "the others recur, bringing them the groundwork, the solid consistency of a rich orchestration" (*GW*, 543).

Orchestration: life can be like music—indeed like beautiful music—if we let it. And that's why we need art; that's why we need septets and novels, not just noises and biographies. If we want our lives to have the richness, complexity, and shape of a classical composition, we'd better listen to some symphonies. If we want to notice recurring motifs as they pop up in our experience, maybe we should take in a bit of Wagner. If we want to recognize a sequence of events as a beautiful story, it helps to spend some time around novels. Art can be a formal model for the shape of a life.

Chapter 8
Intellect and intuition

Proust's novel fairly teems with references to two aspects of the mind, a conscious and an unconscious part. Does that mean Proust is a Freudian? While the hypothesis may seem highly tempting, there's just one pesky little fact in the way: Proust never read a word of Freud.

An unconscious without Freud

My students are often amazed when I tell them that. Doesn't Proust's narrator talk about the unconscious? A lot? Doesn't he say things like "I did not believe that she would have left the house without telling me, but my unconscious thought so" (*C*, 494), "my attention…explored my unconscious" (*TR*, 274), or "our unconscious was therefore more clairvoyant than ourselves at that moment" (*F*, 582)? Doesn't he refer to "the other M. de Charlus, the subconscious one" (*TR*, 247-8)? Doesn't he mention "those symptoms which the doctor hears his patient describe to him and with the help of which he works back to a deeper cause of which the patient is unaware," and go on to claim that "similarly our impressions, our ideas, have only a symptomatic value" (*F*, 756-7)? Didn't Proust himself say that "while reading myself, I have elicited after the fact some constitutive features of my unconscious" and wonder, about Flaubert, "how much effort must have been required to fix that vision properly, to move it out of the unconscious and into the conscious" (*EA*, 288)? How on earth could Proust and his narrator use language like this if Proust was blissfully unaware of Viennese psychology?

The answer is simple: Freud did not invent, or discover, the unconscious. Instead, large numbers of intellectuals were already discussing the idea, and even using the term, far earlier. An entire book on the subject, helpfully titled *Philosophy of the Unconscious*, came out some three decades before *The Interpretation of Dreams*. Arthur Schopenhauer, whose work Proust did know, had a lot to say—in 1818—about humans being driven by inner forces beyond their understanding. Friedrich Nietzsche had his own brilliant observations to throw in about unconscious thought, repression, and inadvertent self-revelation. Early neurologist Jean-Martin Charcot noted that the unconscious produces symptoms. And when Proust says in his 1913 interview that he's writing "a sequence of novels of the unconscious," he does not add that this makes it Freudian; he adds that this makes it in some ways "Bergsonian" (*EA*, 254). (Henri Bergson believed in the importance of unconscious forces, because, well, pretty much everyone did.)

So there *is* an unconscious in Proust, but it isn't one borrowed from Freud. Freudians might of course say it doesn't matter, since if Freud's theories are correct, then they'll apply to Proust's characters just as much as to anyone else. And it's certainly the case that Proust's protagonist has an unusual degree of attachment to his mother; he even thinks of her goodnight kisses—rather disconcertingly for many readers—when he embraces Albertine. Doesn't that mean Proust's novel is a place where every boy harbors a repressed fantasy of killing his father and sleeping with his mother, where such childhood family dynamics carry over into adult relationships, and where our love objects are all just "mother-surrogates"?

I'm not so sure. Swann is tormented and possessive in love too, but he doesn't think of his mother when kissing Odette, and his neurosis, as the narrator explicitly tells us, has a different etiology: "to him that anguish came through love ... but when, as had befallen me, it possesses one's soul before love has yet entered into one's life, then it must drift, awaiting love's coming, vague and free" (*S*, 39–40). The narrator's "anguish" begins in childhood, Swann's in adulthood. There's no reason to assume that everyone in the novel is like the narrator, and in fact good reason to believe otherwise.

Even in the narrator's case, there's no clear evidence that the anguish results from feelings about his mother. An alternative possibility, offered by Georges Poulet, is that it actually predates the drama of the goodnight kiss, and causes it rather than being caused by it. The fraught romantic relationships would then trace their origin to something like an innate individual predisposition, not to ostensibly universal Freudian desires; that would explain why the narrator says misunderstandings in romantic relationships affect "a deeper layer of the heart" (*C*, 108) than those between parents and children.

None of that means, of course, that we *can't* use Freud to understand Proust; but it does mean, I think, that we don't have to.

Two sides of the mind

No Freud, then, but plenty about the unconscious, often referred to as the "instinct" or "intuition." And plenty, in particular, about its interplay with "intellect," the conscious side of the mind. Sometimes the two fight; sometimes they ignore each other; sometimes they work hand in hand. (Pretty much like me and my siblings in years gone by, with the possible exception of the third option.)

One important example of conflict is knowledge of the world, where—as we saw in chapter 5—intellect battles with, and defeats, the distortions of intuition. But the clearest case is knowledge of other people: if you're trying to figure out what's going on in the head of someone you care about, your mind tends to go to two extremes at once, intellect offering a series of soft-focus fairytales, instinct cooking up horror stories to scare you out of your seat. (Neither, you'll recall, is entirely to be trusted.)

This goes double if you're harboring suspicions about your love partner. At that point instinct turns into a veritable sea-monster, bent on your destruction—"thus, like an evil deity, his jealousy inspired Swann, driving him on towards his ruin" (*S*, 518)—while intellect does what it can to keep you calm (and, if necessary, blissfully ignorant). A will to serenity does despairing battle with a will to pain.

The most interesting situations, though, are those where intellect and intuition unwittingly join forces. The special kind of self-deception we heard about at the end of chapter 5—the paradoxical conscious kind—is possible only because intellect believes while, simultaneously, intuition doubts. The self-knowledge we heard about is possible only because intuition reliably distorts the world and then intellect, working back from what it perceives, figures out the sort of person you must be to see things in that special way. (Not to mention the sort of person you must be to love the people you do.)

The theory of art we encountered in chapter 7 functions similarly, with intuition registering "impressions" and intellect turning them into "expressions," poems or plays or prose that can be shared. All we start with, the narrator says, is a set of inarticulate inner pictures; without intellect, we could never translate these into words. Or in another of his lovely metaphors, all we start with is a set of photographic negatives, negatives which "remain useless [if] the intellect has not developed them" (*TR*, 299).

How about involuntary memory, our friend from chapter 3? That too could be a case of inadvertent collaboration. What we saw back then is that when you experience something, your mind divides up the information it's going to store away. (This is an idea Proust drew, perhaps, from Bergson.) There's a part it suspects it may later be able to use "for its own rational purposes" (*TR*, 260); that part is made available to voluntary memory, also known as "the memory of the intellect" (*S*, 59). You can access it deliberately and whenever you want. Everything else, by contrast, ends up in a big dusty storeroom, more or less unfindable, hidden under piles of "pointless" material: "days in the past cover up little by little those that preceded them and are themselves buried beneath those that follow them" (*F*, 733).

If someone asks you who accompanied you on that trip to Balbec, for example, you can easily answer that it was your grandmother: that's an objectively useful piece of information. But how it felt when she helped you take off your boots—that's something you've long forgotten, something deeply buried, something you'll rediscover only by chance and only if you're lucky. A tiny book stashed deep in an enormous cobwebbed library.

So one way to understand what's going on is that intuition allows us to remember the boots that intellect made us forget. And intellect did us a favor in making us forget them, because now they come back to us in a special way, bringing with them the sensations and emotions of a bygone age, a time capsule, even a different self. "Owing to the work of oblivion, the returning memory...causes us suddenly to breathe a new air" (*TR*, 261).

Sometimes, then, unconscious forces can torment us with the nightmare scenarios they concoct. Sometimes they tear us apart, thanks to their incessant war with our conscious attitudes. But sometimes the bitter struggle gives way to a collaboration that can transform our existence. We need both; without them there would be no involuntary memory, no self-knowledge, no art—nothing that, for Proust, really makes life worth living.

Chapter 9
True self and total self

If we're constantly torn between conscious and unconscious impulses, how can we achieve any sense of stable identity? The narrator struggles with this kind of question throughout the novel; "my life appeared to me," he says at one point, "as something utterly devoid of the support of an individual, identical and permanent self" (*F*, 802-3). That's a really bad predicament, and a major part of his achievement lies in finding a clever way out of it.

What it takes

The narrator's predicament is actually even worse than it looks, since it isn't just one problem: it's three. Somehow we need to be not just a self but a self that is (1) "individual," (2) "identical," and (3) "permanent." Having a self that's "individual" doesn't necessarily mean wearing a wetsuit to board meetings—we don't all have to become incorrigible eccentrics—but it does mean that your friends should be able to pick you out of a metaphorical lineup, distinguishing you from the mass of humanity. There should be things you do that make them say "that's very *you* of you." ("That's so Helen!") If you're no more than an ant in the anthill, you may well be fully *unified*, but it makes little sense to speak of you having a *self*.

So you need to be different from other people. But you also need to be the same as yourself. You can't be irremediably pulled apart by conflicting impulses, an unholy mess of competing drives.

And then there's the final requirement: you can't be one thing today, another tomorrow, a third the day after. You can certainly change, of course—and you almost certainly *should*: what would a life be that's always exactly the same, from zero years to a hundred? and what would a character be that doesn't adjust when it learns from experience?—but the set of your states has to hang together in some way that makes sense.

That's why, to say it again, Proust's narrator thinks we need (1) a locus of distinction, (2) a degree of coherence in a moment, and (3) a measure of wholeness across time. This triple achievement is something people have been interested in for centuries—the ancient Stoics, for example, had remarkably smart things to say about it—but the modern world may well have given it added urgency. Ever since the late Middle Ages, increasing numbers of individuals have gained the freedom to decide who and what to be; their identity is no longer given to them at birth, as it might once have been ("you're the son of the smith, and that means you have to shoe horses"). In Proust, as we saw in chapter 6, even a bastion of traditionalism like high society can end up becoming unstable. So decisions about what to do—about who to be—can't be settled for any of us (thank goodness) by membership in a class, a guild, a religion, or a nation. Each of us is on our own. What are we to do?

Why it matters

Before we answer that, let's take a step back and ask why it's worth answering in the first place. Why should anyone want a sense of stable identity, complete with distinction, coherence, and wholeness? Isn't the notion of distinction just a dangerous illusion, making us prisoners of our own vanity? Even if you don't think *that*, isn't it far better to be multiple and protean than to be coherent and whole? ("I am large, I contain multitudes": Walt Whitman's line can sound pretty appealing at times.) So why not embrace internal complexity and constant change? Why not choose to leave yourself as a chaotic jumble of fragments?

This is a very complicated question with a very long history, and there are powerful arguments for the no-self position (not least from the side of Buddhist philosophy). But there are also one or two decent arguments in the other direction, explaining why many of us want at least *some* sense of distinction, some degree of coherence in our character, and some measure of wholeness in our life. We've already seen Proust's narrator offering a lovely reason for coherence and distinction, in the form of re-enchantment: human beings are different, and difference is awe-inspiring. "With people like these we do really fly from star to star." Other people are a wonder of the world!…but only if there are actual selves.

There's also the issue of decision-making. If you're just a big mess, rather than a reasonably harmonious character, then you may have trouble choosing what to do. (Which part of you gets the final say?) You'll often be conflicted; like Hamlet, you may end up either doing nothing or doing something impulsive, something you're not committed to, something you may later come to regret. If you want your actions to be *yours*, there'd better be a "you" for them to belong to.

What about unity across time? Why might it be helpful for me to think of my life hanging together as a single complicated story, rather than a series of lives lived by a bunch of successive Joshes? Proust's narrator offers an interesting answer to that. "The memory of the most multiple person," he says, "establishes a sort of identity in him and makes him reluctant to go back on promises which he remembers, even if he has not countersigned them" (*TR*, 3). If some bloke named Josh Landy promises his partner he'll travel to the frozen wastes for the holidays and then, in December, doesn't feel like it any more, he can't just say he's a different person now. ("Sorry, but 'life is made up of a perpetual renewal of cells,' just like Proust's narrator says (*F*, 802). That promiser bloke was a whole other person!") Holding ourselves to our commitments depends on accepting past versions of us as *us*. And the same goes for holding ourselves responsible for our actions. Who wants to live in a world where no one feels accountable for anything they've done or said?

Likewise for all the future Joshes. I *could* think of them as a bunch of random strangers, with nothing to do with me or with each other; but I'm not sure that would really be the best idea. Let's say you've got a marathon coming up in two months, so you decide to skip dessert tonight. Why skip that dessert if the future marathon-runner isn't really *you*? Thinking of your future as *your* future can help you make and keep plans, motivating you to trade short-term sacrifices for long-term achievements. Just as you should probably take responsibility for your past, so it's probably smart to take ownership of your future. You'll feel properly embarrassed about lousy stuff you did, properly satisfied about good stuff you did, properly keen to avoid things going wrong, and properly excited to see how things turn out. How things turn out for *you*, the same person doing the remembering and lamenting and planning and day-dreaming right now.

Plus there are other advantages to securing a sense of wholeness across time, a sense that your various incarnations (you at twenty, you at thirty, you at forty...) are chapters in a single story, rather than a library's worth of books about separate characters. In chapter 7 we learned that a story is more than the sum of its parts: it's not just a series of episodes but also the overall shape they collectively form (rags to riches? seeking to finding? error to understanding? rise to fall?), the overall feeling they collectively produce (triumph? relief? dejection?), the overall value they collectively contain (a life you'd choose? a life you'd avoid?). If you

Marcel Proust

86

can see your existence as an unfolding narrative, you can figure out whether it's really the life you want—in time, ideally, to change course.

Let me add just one last reason for wanting wholeness. A fascinating fact about stories is that later events can reach back and change the significance of earlier events. Normally we assume that events come with their significance built in: winning the lottery is always a good thing, and having a toothache is always a bad thing. But what if you happen to meet the love of your life in the dentist's waiting room? All of a sudden that pain in the molar becomes, retrospectively, a periodontic godsend.

Something very similar happens right at the end of Proust's novel. The narrator has finally figured out how to write his book, and he suddenly comes to appreciate his physical frailty: "ill health," he explains, "by compelling me, like a severe director of conscience, to die to the world, had done me a favor" (*TR*, 526). If he hadn't become so weak, he would have continued spending (i.e. wasting) his free hours in society, and would have had no time to do his writing; infirmity proves, in a way, to be the best thing that ever happened to him. (In an earlier draft, the narrator is even more explicit, saying "perhaps I should bless my poor health, which has taught me … stillness, silence, the possibility of working" (*1908*, 60-1).) This is the amazing magic of narrative, which sometimes allows us—without self-deception!—to see our setbacks and challenges in a whole new light. But that magic only works if we think of our life as a story.

Why it's difficult

Hopefully it's now clear why the narrator cares so much about having a measure of distinction, coherence, and wholeness. (Though again, it's fair enough if you disagree with him, especially if you're a Buddhist.) But assuming we want that, what's the problem? Why is it hard to be who we are?

We've already encountered a couple of the reasons. In chapter 7 we saw that conformity is a danger to distinction: even Vinteuil sometimes fails to be himself, caving in to the desire to pander to his audience. And in chapter 8 we saw that internal division is a threat to coherence. Our mind often finds itself split into two warring factions, intellect and intuition, optimism and pessimism, faith and doubt, fear and hope.

(Since I just mentioned chapters 7 and 8, now might well be a good moment to say that you'll see cross-references like that dotted throughout this chapter. That's deliberate: the reflections on selfhood in Proust are both fascinating and complex, so I've tried to put some building blocks in place before trying to assemble a self-shaped house out of them. Here and there I'll insert a reminder or two, indicating where you can find longer discussions of quickly made points. But if they're not helpful, please feel free to pretend they don't exist.)

We can add, too, that each of us has multiple facets to our character, which Proust's narrator typically calls "aspects." Take for example Rachel, the woman Robert de Saint-Loup is madly in love with. The narrator first met her while she was working in a brothel; now, however, she is an actress of "great talent" (*GW*, 222). Contrary to a certain cultural bias in our society, it isn't true to say that Rachel is only "superficially" a great actress but "really" someone who once worked in a brothel. She's genuinely both. "What we believed to be a thing with one definite aspect," says the narrator in a different context, contains a "hundred other things which it may equally well be, since each is related to a no less legitimate perspective" (*GW*, 499).

Proust's novel is full of wonderful recognition scenes. (Jump to the next paragraph if you want to avoid spoilers.) As we just saw, Robert's actress girlfriend Rachel turns out to be the same Rachel we came across before, the one who worked in a brothel. Meanwhile the "lady in pink," glamorous companion of great-uncle Adolphe, turns out to have been...Odette! And the man engaging in sexual play at a seedy hotel turns out to be, of all people, the distinguished Baron de Charlus! It's the same person who returns in each case, but in a different guise. That's partly because we change, but it's also partly because only one side of us is visible at a time. Each of us is more than meets the immediate eye.

So much for threats to distinction and coherence. What about wholeness? Here the answer is simple: you're not the same person you were at age five, nor the same person you will be at age ninety-five. "I had always considered each one of us to be a sort of multiple organism," the narrator says, "not only at a given moment of time...but also...as a sequence of juxtaposed but distinct 'I's which would die one after the other" (*TR, 352*).

He uses this metaphor a lot—an old self "dying," a new self being "born"—to capture just how different we feel from one stage of our lives to another. It's difficult to understand our past behavior, he says, because we were a different person then; and we can't predict our future behavior, because we will be a different person again. ("In myself, too, many things have perished which I imagined would last forever, and new ones have arisen, giving birth to new sorrows and new joys I could not have foreseen, just as now the old are hard to understand" (*S, 49*).) Oh, and we change a lot of times. The " 'selves' that compose our personality," we're told, are "innumerable" (*F, 579*). We "die" and get "reborn" not every decade but every year, every month, maybe every day.

And it gets even worse (or better, depending on your point of view). Those ostensibly "dead" selves never really go away; they stick around like ghosts, haunting your mind and your decisions. To use a more Proustian metaphor, the various selves are like layers of rock inside a volcano, each ready to get flung to the top. ("Our self is composed of the superimposition of our successive states. But this superimposition is not unalterable like the

89

stratification of a mountain. Incessant upheavals raise to the surface ancient deposits" (F, 733).) If you don't like that visual image, think of each self as driving the bus for a while, then being ousted and sent to the back; at that point they no longer do the steering, but they still get to yell out where they want to go, and all of them have an equal vote. If enough former selves insist on us driving out to the frozen wastes in December, I guess we'd better pack a jacket.

A true self

That's a complicated picture of selfhood, but it's quite a powerful one in many respects, offering explanations for a bunch of phenomena. One of my favorites is recovery from grief or heartbreak. How on earth do we bounce back from rejection, or loss, when nothing in the external world changes? We still have feelings for a person, and they are still no longer in our life, so why not remain as inconsolable after five years as we are after five days?

The answer has to do with the idea we just heard, about those unruly passengers in the bus. All you have to do is spend time doing other things, and gradually you will accumulate passengers who are not constantly thinking about the loss. Pretty soon the indifferent passengers come to outnumber (and outvote) the grief-stricken, and before you know it you're driving to an amusement park rather than to the nearest bar. "We must seek to encourage these thoughts," says Proust's narrator, "to make them grow, while the sentiment which is no more now than a memory dwindles, so that the new elements introduced into the mind contest with that sentiment, wrest from it an ever-increasing portion of our soul, until at last the victory is complete" (BG, 285).

And better yet, there are actually solutions on hand to the problems we began with, the problems of distinction, coherence,

Marcel Proust appears in the left margin

and wholeness. (Here we're going to start putting together a large number of things we've seen along the way—proving, I hope, that you haven't just wasted a perfectly good afternoon.) The first solution is your "true self." We saw that this true self is "awakened" during moments of involuntary memory. We saw that it's usually hidden, being totally different from the mask you put on while in society. And we saw that it's something like a perspective, a conceptual scheme, an idiosyncratic way of processing what you experience. That's why it's responsible for the connections you make while enjoying an impression, like that of three steeples at sunset.

But it's also responsible for the style of your writing and, to some extent, of your speech. It drives your choice of love partner, the unique way you react to a piece of art, and even some of the general theories you form about life. Because of all that, you can gather information about it, not by introspection but by "working back" from what you notice yourself doing, whether while reading, while writing, while thinking, or while in love. And you can learn to imbue more and more of your art and life with it, essentially by getting out of your own way.

What we can now add is that this "true self" offers a partial solution to all three problems. First of all, it makes us significantly different from other people. Second, it speaks in one voice; whatever hectic squabbles are going on inside your head, it's like the quiet study you can retreat to, with a good lock on the door. And finally, it doesn't change over the years but is instead, as the narrator says, a "being...outside time" (*TR*, 262).

This leads to a rather lovely irony. Proust's narrator won't stop going on about how everything is constantly changing, how he's "died" numerous times in the course of his life, how he can't imagine thinking what he once thought and wanting what he once wanted, how his successive selves are so different they should have different names...and yet his style almost never varies. Those majestic sentences, often fearsomely long and fiendishly convoluted but always masterfully controlled; that tentativeness, those qualifications; that play with time and tenses; those scenes of stunning recognition—this is writing you could pick out of a line-up, any day of the week. And the narrator himself, as we know, sees consistency of artistic style as evidence for the stability of selfhood: all composers, he says, have "a distinctive strain the sameness of which—for whatever its subject it remains identical with itself—proves the permanence of the elements that compose [their] soul" (*C*, 342-3). So even as he tells us the self is irremediably fragmented and unstable and inconsistent, he does so in a style that proves exactly the reverse.

A harmonious self

So the true self gives you coherence, wholeness, and distinction: it's unitary; it never changes; and it sets you apart. Oh, and as a nice side-benefit, it re-enchants the world. That's not bad...but it's not everything. The true self may well be the *essence* of who you are—"this essence," the narrator says, "was me" (*S*, 60)—but it isn't the *whole* of who you are.

Intellect and intuition are still duking it out. Plus, temporal selves are still accumulating like crazy in the back of the bus, and they too are an important part of you. (Memories of old rooms "put together," says the narrator, "the component parts of my self" (*S*, 4); "all this length of Time...was in fact me" (*TR*, 530-1).) So aren't you still a mess, mostly speaking?

Proust's narrator doesn't say anything explicit about this question, and neither, as far as I know, does Proust. But I think we can glimpse a solution or two between the lines. Intellect and intuition, implacable foes when it comes to jealousy, can be made to work together—perhaps in spite of themselves—toward a common goal. Remember what we saw in chapter 8: great art depends on both, if the narrator is right, as do self-understanding, conscious self-deception, and maybe even involuntary memory.

This is a special way to be unified, one where the divisions continue to exist. Think of a healthy democracy, where many parties and religions and lifestyles go together to form a single nation. Or better, think of a car. Your car has an engine that makes it go and a braking system that makes it stop, but only the most hardened (non-Buddhist) skeptic would say "your Audi is just a mass of fragments, not a car!" A braking system doesn't have remotely the same job as an engine; it isn't *like* an engine; and we don't *attempt* to make the two things similar. (That would be bad news for your Audi—don't try it at home.) Rather, the two very different parts, along with the pistons and axles and valves and spark plugs, go together to produce a combined overall effect: getting you from point A to point B.

That's also how it is, perhaps, for the systems in your mind. Intellect doesn't do the same thing as intuition; it isn't like intuition; and we don't try to make it similar to intuition. You can't get the two to agree—but if you work hard enough, you can trick them into collaborating. That, I think, is the situation we find Proust's protagonist in at the end of *Time Regained*, as he starts to write his novel: he's discovered a true self which is consistently unitary, and his character as a whole is unified *by the goal it tends toward*, like a complicated car driving in a single direction.

The sixteenth-century philosopher Michel de Montaigne had an even better analogy to offer. "In a concert of instruments," he wrote, "we do not hear a lute, a spinet, and the flute; we hear a rounded harmony, the effect of various elements joined into a whole." Our task is to take the various parts of our character, each singing a different note, and turn them into a single beautiful chord. It's a good thing, not a bad thing, that they aren't all middle C.

A narrative self

OK, but all those passengers in your mental bus—you at age five, you at age fifteen, you at age twenty-five...—what are you supposed to do with *them*? (Other than, to paraphrase *Jaws*, getting a bigger bus?) The solution here is actually quite similar. The idea is not that your various selves are identical (they aren't). Or that you can *make* them identical (you can't). Rather, the idea is that you can take those many selves and turn them into a single *story*, where, as with your car, the assorted components join together to get you from A to B.

This goes back to something that came up earlier: a story is more than the sum of its parts. As we saw in chapter 7, a narrative is not only a series of exploits and experiences but also the overall shape they collectively form, the overall impact they collectively produce, and the overall value they collectively contain. So if you can picture your life as a story, rather than just as a set of disjointed episodes, then it starts to hang together; instead of being twenty million random fragments, it feels like one thing, something you can give an overarching name to ("rags to riches," "rise and fall," "successful quest"). Suddenly you can think about the twenty million selves at once, assess them as a whole, carry them around in your pocket.

Narrative theorists sometimes tell us there are two ways of recounting a series of events. One, which they call a "chronicle," is basically a list—the sort of thing you'd find in a diary. ("Monday: stayed in and read. Tuesday: binge-watched *The Wire*. Wednesday: ate some toast.") The other, which they call a "narrative," adds a kind of glue, binding the parts together into a single tale, with start, middle, and end. To achieve wholeness over time, then, all you need to do is find your narrative. The chapters may be very different, but together they add up to a book that makes sense.

To be fair, there's no explicit statement along these lines in the *Search*. But then again, you might say that the entire *Search* is a three-thousand-page illustration of it. It is, as the narrator himself says, the story of a vocation (*GW*, 544); it's a spiritual rags-to-riches tale, one in which lost purpose, lost connection, lost identity, lost belonging, and lost enchantment all find themselves miraculously restored. Proust's narrator doesn't tell us his plan is to take the various incidents and phases of his past and turn them into a memoir that makes sense of them, presenting them as stations on the way to the life he wants—instead he just goes ahead and does that, leaving us to draw the necessary conclusions.

None of this means that you have to write a three-thousand-page memoir in order to have a full sense of self. Most of us simply hold that narrative in our heads. (Nobody needs to read the boring story of a tea-loving expat Brit teaching Proust in California!) But if we can keep it available for ourselves, keep it honest and coherent and reasonably complete, and thereby combine a true self with a total self, we'll have joined Proust's narrator in solving one of the big problems of life.

Success and failure

Will we have solved *all* the problems of life? Not in the slightest. Becoming who you are is beneficial for the many reasons we saw above, and ideally it may help you do a good deed or two. (In the narrator's case, it allows him to write a book that is "usable by others" (*TR*, 513), one that brings self-knowledge to its readers and a ray of enchantment into the world.) But it's certainly no guarantee of virtue.

As Proust scholar Antoine Compagnon has pointed out, *In Search of Lost Time* is fascinated by moments of kindness (like the Queen of Naples swooping in to rescue Charlus from humiliation (*C*, 429-33), or Robert de Saint-Loup swooping in to save the narrator from "despair" (*GW*, 538-41)) and moments of malice (like Mme Verdurin turning Charlus's beloved Morel against him to satisfy her own vanity (*C*, 414-24), or Mlle Vinteuil spitting on a photograph of her late father (*S*, 230)). The narrator himself speaks "wounding words" (*BG*, 501 and *SG*, 214) to his ailing grandmother; is at times almost criminally cruel to Albertine, whom he treats—in his own words—as a "prisoner"; stalks the Duchesse; and even appears to be guilty of sexual misconduct. (To be clear, we're still speaking about the narrator, not about Proust.) When it comes to ethics, he is very, very far from a model to be emulated.

To be better than that—to become the kind of individual who radiates kindness and refrains from cruelty—you're going to need more than a harmonious self. Although self-fashioning won't automatically make you a narcissist, let alone a monster, it also won't automatically make you a saint; to be a good person, you have to acquire a set of healthy moral values.

Even if we leave morality aside, there's an awful lot that self-fashioning doesn't do for the narrator. Yes, it gives him identity, authenticity, the power to keep his promises, and something to write about. It also gives him a way to feel better about being sickly, and perhaps about all that time "wasted" in salons as well. But it isn't going to redeem *everything* bad in his life; nor is it going to provide him with connection, purpose, or a sense of belonging. He still needs Vermeer and Bergotte and Elstir and Vinteuil. And he still needs to live with style and to write with art.

Third, when it comes to self-fashioning, it's always possible to *fail*. (That's a point Robert Pippin makes in a hugely important essay.) In Proust's novel, the main character wants to become a writer—but "being a writer" isn't as simple as typing up some pages. He's going to have to get those pages published, for one thing. And they're probably going to have to be halfway decent, for another.

Samuel Beckett illustrates this point with devastating wit in one of his plays, whose protagonist abandons true love to devote himself to literature. The result, thirty years later? "Seventeen copies sold, of which eleven at trade price to free circulating libraries beyond the seas." What's hilarious (and tragic) about this is the next line: "Getting known." The character is absurdly happy and proud about his global total of seventeen sales; he probably thinks he can claim "writer" as his identity. But he's wrong. As Vincent Descombes rightly puts it, "one cannot become a great writer all by oneself." Who you are isn't entirely up to you.

While we're on the subject of what self-fashioning won't do, let's add that it won't make absolutely everything hang together. There will always be false starts, loose threads, dead ends; unity is a matter of degree, not all or nothing. We can never be *perfectly* harmonious (and maybe we don't want to be). But we can be *relatively* harmonious (and for Proust's narrator, we do want that).

Finally, your story can only ever be *provisional*. There's a lovely exchange in *Don Quixote* between the protagonist and a man named Gines de Pasamonte, who happens to be writing his autobiography. Don Quixote asks him if it's finished. "How can it be finished," answers Gines, "if my life isn't?"

As long as you're alive, your story can never be finished. And that doesn't just mean you don't know what's going to happen in the future; it means you don't really know what happened in the past! You know (in many cases) the facts about what happened, but you don't necessarily know their *significance*.

Imagine you write your memoirs, right now, and send them off for publication. Then, two weeks after they come out, you run into someone who went to the same high school as you, someone you'd totally forgotten about. You get a cup of tea together, then dinner a few days later. You realize you have lots in common. You fall in

97

love, get married, and start living happily ever after. This is great (congratulations by the way), but I think you're going to need a new edition of your autobiography. You'd better rewrite the section about high school, stat. And you will definitely be using the phrase "little did I know." (*There I was, sitting in Math class, trying to figure out linear algebra. Little did I know that the love of my life was sitting right behind me....*)

There's an episode a bit like this in Proust. When the narrator first hears about Albertine, he barely pays any attention, and turns down an opportunity to meet her. (All of his thoughts are focused on Gilberte.) And so, later on, he says something very close to "little did I know": "my love for Albertine...was already inscribed in my love for Gilberte, in the midst of the happy days of which, for the first time, I had heard the name of Albertine pronounced and her character described by her aunt, *without suspecting* that this insignificant seed would develop and would one day overshadow the whole of my life" (*TR*, 312, my emphasis).

In cases like these, the future reaches back and changes the past. It makes the information about Albertine suddenly worth mentioning, the possible encounter with her a painfully missed opportunity. (He might, he explains, have loved Albertine a little sooner, which would "have put an end to [his] present sufferings" (*BG*, 277).) The future causes minor episodes to have been momentous, setbacks to have been stepping-stones, triumphs to have been catastrophes, infirmity to have been the best thing that ever happened to you. The facts stay the same, but their significance turns on its head. And so, to say it again, any story you tell about yourself can only be provisional.

All that said, being provisional is very different from being (automatically) *false*; while self-deception is an ever-present threat, it isn't completely insurmountable. And these narratives

The hidden structure of *Swann's Way*

If you're reading *Swann's Way* right now, please take a moment to appreciate how amazing the structure is. It looks for all the world like a haphazard assortment of random memories, each thrown on the page as soon as it comes to mind. But the apparent stream of consciousness conceals a carefully organized progression.

The first page finds our protagonist completely adrift, lost in half-sleep, no clue who or indeed what he is. Not only is he not a particular individual; he's not human! Or any kind of life form, for that matter. Instead he's just a bunch of minerals (a church)—or maybe an abstract object (a quartet)—or maybe even a *fractured* abstraction (the rivalry between François I and Charles V).

A couple of pages later he is still "more destitute than a caveman" but has at least "the feeling of existence" (*S*, 4): he knows he's a life form, indeed a human life form ... he just doesn't know which one. And then the memories of rooms descend "like a rope let down from heaven" to rescue him, restoring "the original traits of [his] self" (*S*, 4-5). The various people he has been—at Combray, at Balbec, at Doncières—give him a sense of the story of his life, one important half of who he is.

All that's missing now is the other half, the half that's outside of time. And that's on its way. The madeleine indicates the existence of a true self; and then, a hundred or so pages later, some of its details get filled in by means of the steeples passage, impression completing the work done by involuntary memory.

Proust often insisted to correspondents that, in spite of appearances, his book had a deliberate shape and plan. It certainly changed a lot over the years, and it would be a vast exaggeration to say that everything fits a perfect pattern. But in many ways he was right—and this, I think, is one of them.

are helpful—maybe even vital. They won't be perfect, and they won't solve every problem you have, but they'll still do you some really great favors. If you want to choose wisely and take responsibility and steer your future and redeem your setbacks, maybe you shouldn't give up on them just yet. Partial, provisional, and precarious as they are, those stories are essential to a life well lived.

Chapter 10
Why a novel?

You've nearly finished this book, and it's time for me to admit that quite a lot of it has been about theories. We've heard what Proust's narrator has to tell us about involuntary memory, impressions, love, knowledge, selfhood, authorship, and art. We've also heard what Proust himself had to say, in his own name, about some of those things, while writing his essays and correspondence. I personally think all of that is fascinating. But it doesn't explain an equally fascinating fact: that Proust spent the last decade of his life, and then some, composing a gigantic *novel*, not a philosophy manual. So why did he do that? What's so special about fiction?

"Am I a novelist?"

When Proust chose literature over philosophy, it's unlikely he did so by flipping a coin. In 1908, he was clearly thinking hard about which form of writing to go for, and dropped a line to Anna de Noailles to ask for advice: the manuscript he was working on would either begin with "the story of a morning" or be a "traditional essay," and he wanted her to help him decide. And in a notebook from the same year, a voice wonders aloud "should I make a novel out of it, [or] a philosophical study; am I a novelist?" (*1908*, 61)

When you think how much Proust and his narrator had to say about what art can do and other things can't—all those wonderful benefits we heard about in chapter 7—that makes it even weirder to imagine he decided at random. Instead it seems more likely that he took his own advice. A treatise, he knew, can offer claims and arguments, but a novel can (also) transmit its author's perspective, help its reader learn about herself, show us the dreamworld we live in as human beings, and offer templates for self-fashioning. "His world," "my world," "our world," formal models: could all of that be why Proust selected fiction over non-fiction, "the story of a morning" over the "traditional essay"?

A Rorschach test

Way back in chapter 4, we saw that Swann falls in love with Odette "for the first time" over and over again, for all kinds of different and contradictory reasons. We're told that Swann falls for Odette because she's affectionate, and certain to love him back; but we're also told that Swann falls for Odette because she's remote, and unlikely to love him back. Elsewhere we're told that it's because Odette's face resembles a figure in a Botticelli painting; elsewhere still, because Vinteuil's sonata made Swann susceptible to tender feelings. Why on earth would Proust set things up this way?

Hervé Picherit offers an ingenious answer. Almost all of us, he says, will subliminally pick one of these options—painting, music, anxiety, recommendation, affection—and that choice should tell us something about ourselves. If you're a romantic, you'll be more likely to have zeroed in on the Botticelli or the sonata. If you're a cynic, you'll be more likely to have focused on the anxiety. If you said it's because Odette makes a great cup of tea, chances are you're a Brit like myself.

So Proust's novel, just like the narrator's future book, works as an "optical instrument," helping us to be "the readers of [our] own selves." By setting a little interpretive trap, it offers us a way to learn things we didn't necessarily know about our minds. If we spend enough time around Proust, we may well come to realize that *Swann in Love* was more complicated than we first assumed; this, in turn, may make us wonder why we assumed differently; and once we're there, we're in a position "to discern what, without this book, we would perhaps never have perceived in ourselves." The book has done us the wonderful favor of acting like a Rorschach test—something a "traditional essay" could never have done.

The feeling of what happens

Proust's novel gives me a bit of "my world," then, and you a bit of "your world." It may also give both of us "his world": perhaps the style of the novel hints at the idiosyncratic vision of Proust, just as "Miss Sacripant" transmits Elstir's. (Maybe we're only seeing the *narrator's* true self, to be fair, but the possibility of detecting a smidgen of Proust's is not completely ruled out.) And whether or not Proust's world is on offer here, *our* world definitely is. On multiple occasions and by multiple means, the novel helps us feel what it's like to experience something—in ways we haven't necessarily noticed, consciously, while going about our lives.

"A little tap on the window-pane, as though something had struck it, followed by a plentiful light falling sound, as of grains of sand being sprinkled from a window overhead, gradually spreading, intensifying, acquiring a regular rhythm, becoming fluid, sonorous, musical, immeasurable, universal: it was the rain" (*S*, 140-1). The novel is full of beautiful moments like this— moments where it tricks us like an optical illusion does, capturing the way in which reality appears to us rather than the way it is, the effect it produces on our senses rather than whatever it was that caused it. Moments where Proust's novel might as well be a landscape (or is it seascape?) by Elstir.

(Can novels do what Elstir-type paintings can? Yes! Proust's narrator repeatedly compares Elstir to Dostoevsky (*BG*, 315; *C*, 510; *TR*, 431).)

Hearing rain as sand is an auditory illusion we'll correct within instants, but sometimes our ill-adjusted brains make mistakes that take days or weeks to fix, like that mole on Albertine's chin—sorry, I mean her cheek—that we talked about in chapter 4. (Sorry again, I mean her lip.) Again, we're being given the *feeling of what it's like* to get the world wrong, in the kind of way that's common to the entire human species.

And this may apply not only to factual errors (like "Albertine's mole is on her lip") but also to philosophical mistakes (like "our souls survive after we die"). Early on, Proust's narrator professes to find "very reasonable" the "Celtic belief that the souls of those whom we have lost are held captive in some inferior being, in an animal, in a plant, in some inanimate object" (*S*, 59); by the end, though, he's declaring decisively that there's no life after death (*TR*, 524). Maybe what we've witnessed, then, is the "evolution of a belief system"—exactly the thing Proust told Jacques Rivière he was trying to recreate in his novel. Maybe we're feeling *what it's like* to get not just facts wrong but our theories too, and then to get those theories wrong again in a different way, and then a little bit less wrong (but still not entirely right) after 3,000 long pages....

Three ways, then, in which Proust's novel delivers the phenomenology of human experience: what it's like, first, when our senses get an initial fuzzy grasp on incoming sensations ("grains of sand being sprinkled from a window"); what it's like, second, when our brains try to store the visual image of a person (chin, cheek, lip); what it's like, third, as our intellect makes its long, meandering march toward the truth.

The feeling of remembering

And there may also be a fourth, which would arguably be the best of all. What if Proust's novel simulates the experience of involuntary memory, precisely by being so insanely long? That's a lovely idea one or two commentators have hinted at. Let me try to illustrate it by means of an example.

Early in volume 2, we find the narrator in love with Gilberte, and we learn an apparently trivial detail about the signature on a letter she mails him: "the elaborate capital 'G' leaning against the undotted 'i' looked more like an 'A,' while the final syllable was indefinitely prolonged by a waving flourish" (*BG*, 101). Since this detail is clearly unimportant, we forget about it. Or rather, we *half* forget about it. Two thousand pages later, Gilberte asks a clerk to send the narrator a telegram which she's signed with her name—Gilberte with a Gi that looks like an A, making "Alberte"; Alberte with an indefinitely prolonged final syllable, making... "Albertine" (*F*, 889). The result is an incident that's truly amazing, for reasons I won't spoil here.

This scene gives me goosebumps every time I reread it. There's a crazy "aha" feeling as we realize that a totally insignificant fact reported two thousand pages earlier was actually a crucial setup for an incredibly powerful payoff. And there's a flood of associated memories that return along with it: the letter Gilberte sent, what that letter meant to the narrator, what happened before that made it so important to him, what happened afterwards as a result of it, the hopes it implied, the fate of those hopes....

Clearly we stored that information away, then, but not in a place we could have found it deliberately. (If someone had asked us to describe Gilberte's signature, we wouldn't have known what they were talking about.) It was too random and inconsequential, and so—as we already saw the narrator say with regard to involuntary memory—"our intellect, having no use for it, had rejected [it]" (*BG*, 300). Lucky us! It's that half-forgetting that makes the scene so powerful when it returns. That's precisely the feeling of involuntary memory.

If that's true, then it's a really delightful effect of the novel. By the penultimate volume, even those readers who've never felt the full force of an involuntary memory, or perhaps never experienced one at all, will now have a sense, at least approximately, of what it might be like if they did. Not even the greatest philosophy book could hope to pull that off.

The shape of a life

What's on offer in Proust, then, is not just *the* world—which would also have been available in a treatise-style philosophy book—but also perhaps *his* world, very likely *our* world, and almost certainly *my* world (which is to say, *your* world). Those were the first four benefits of art we discussed in chapter 7. But what about the fifth? Can Proust's novel, like Vinteuil's septet, serve as a formal model for the shape of a life?

I tend to believe it can. At the end of chapter 7, we saw that there are two ways to stitch together episodes and make a life story. One is by thinking of those episodes as something like an engine, where the fuel powers the motor and the motor drives the pistons and the pistons move the wheels. This is story as chain of causes and effects: Emma Bovary's unfortunate reading diet *causes* her inaccurate picture of love, which *causes* her poor decisions, which in turn…etc.

The other way to stitch episodes together is by treating them like a piece of music. The early notes don't cause the later notes but instead *pave the way* for them, foreshadow them, and combine with them to form a symphony that, taken all in all, is a thing of beauty and power.

The story we see in Proust's novel is of the second kind. It starts out pretty inauspiciously, with the narrator fretting madly over a goodnight kiss, trying and failing to find love, and undergoing endless writer's block. It concludes, of course, in triumph—but the triumph isn't *caused* by the years of suffering. It's not because the narrator was a miserable child in *Combray*, a miserable adolescent in *Place Names: The Name*, and a miserable adult in *The Captive* that ends up finding his vocation as an artist in *Time Regained*. (His future book will be *about* his life, but it isn't the result of it.) Instead he gets lucky, thanks to the series of involuntary memories that rain down upon him the day of the Guermantes reception.

So how *do* the earlier and later parts hang together? Well, by forming a single story with a single shape and a single overarching impact. As we saw in chapter 9, it's a rags-to-riches story of the soul. The inner rags didn't *cause* the inner riches, just as the start of the septet didn't cause its finale, but together they produce a rising curve (shape) and a feeling of triumph (impact). Despair plus serenity equals salvation.

And this is a shape we ourselves can borrow when we think about our own lives. Are you happy with where you are now, but sad about (or ashamed of) your humble beginnings? You're missing out! Leaving the content of Proust's novel where it is, lift out the *shape*, and see what happens when you lay it, like a dress pattern, over the events you've witnessed and actions you've performed. As long as your early actions were merely embarrassing, rather than criminal or despicable, you should be *glad* they are part of the story you tell yourself and others. "The picture of what we were at an earlier stage," says Elstir, "cannot, certainly, be pleasing to contemplate in later life. But we must not repudiate it, for it is a proof…that we have, from the common elements of life…extracted something that transcends them" (*BG*, 606).

So we can use Proust's novel—the shape of the story it tells—to guide our picture of our *own* life, helping us, potentially, to come to terms with our past. And we can, perhaps, even use the individual *sentences* a similar way. Many of those sentences are notoriously long and convoluted, but they aren't just chaotic stream-of-consciousness ramblings. Instead they tend to be highly organized machines, collecting things that belong together, separating things that belong apart, and classifying everything under a hierarchy of significance. (The sentence about the septet, reproduced in chapter 7, is itself a perfect example.) And so they too offer a model for us, showing us how to take the crazy mass of thoughts and memories and doubts and hypotheses in our heads and shape them into structures that keep them manageable, even when we can't be certain or decisive or single-minded.

Is it too far-fetched to imagine that we're being invited to do with Proust what his narrator did with Vinteuil? That we're being invited not to behave like Proust's character—his actions are sometimes unconscionable—but rather to think in the shape of a Proustian sentence, and live in the shape of a Proustian novel?

Flexing your mental muscles

There's one last thing, or set of things, Proust's novel may be doing. Fair warning: this part's going to be particularly speculative. With "the world," "our world," "his world," and "my world," our speculations sat on pretty solid ground—we just had to apply to Proust's novel what its narrator himself says about art—and for the formal model idea we had at least the septet passage to go on. Here, though, we're more or less on our own. That said, I don't think what I'm about to suggest is completely crazy; see what you decide.

In Search of Lost Time is not a quick read. It's also not an *easy* read, thanks in part to the famously intricate sentences, many of which need multiple stabs before we figure them out. And to top it all, as we saw in chapter 4, the narrator isn't always reliable. Each of these formal features—unreliability, intricacy, length—contributes to the *experience* we have when reading Proust. And each of them (as we also saw in chapter 4) prompts a certain kind of mental activity, indeed a certain kind of mental *work*. Why? What's in it for us to struggle so hard and for so long?

One thing is for sure: it can't just be for the sake of knowledge. If Proust had merely had nuggets of wisdom to impart, he could simply have written that essay he was thinking of in 1908; that would have saved us all a lot of time, not to mention spared us all a lot of confusion. He could have spoken in his own voice, rather than in the voice of an only semi-reliable narrator, and made it very clear, on every question, exactly what he believed. But he didn't. The *Search* fairly buries us under an avalanche of theories, some true, some half-true, some right for the wrong reasons, some completely false, and almost none of them marked with a handy Alice-in-Wonderland-style label ("accept me!" "reject me!"). We are the ones who have to decide.

Why go the confusing route? Three possible reasons, all of which I think are true. The first, already proposed a couple of sections ago, is that a book like this may convey what it feels like to grope one's way toward illumination. (Remember Proust's lovely line to Jacques Rivière: "I did not want to analyze this evolution of a belief system abstractly, but rather to recreate it.")

The second reason involves something we saw in chapter 4: on Proust's view, books are positively dangerous when people treat them as gospels, mistakenly thinking truth is "deposited between the leaves of books like honey." A book like the *Search*—a story narrated by a character who changes his mind, contradicts himself, and says things the novel proves false—should, in theory, be harder to treat as a gospel. (Though, alas, some scholars have managed it anyway.)

The third, and most interesting, is that it serves as a training-ground for our mind.

That insanely long novel, full of tiny seeds that flower hundreds or thousands of pages later? It encourages us to stretch our memory capacity. We get in the habit of socking away data before we can know how or even whether it's important. (The narrator does exactly that with Albertine: once he comes to realize that she frequently contradicts herself, he gets in the habit of retaining every little thing she says.) Even at the level of a single page, those famous sentences often do something similar, forcing us to hold their early clauses in our head for an unusually lengthy spell, just so as to make sense of everything by the time we get to the end.

That unreliability? Sooner or later it's bound to change our attitude to the material we receive. We're not just invited to file away a large amount of information; we're invited to store some of it in quotation marks, under advisement, aware that it's been delivered to us by a person who's been wrong before and may well be wrong again. We attach a *probabilistic value* to what we hear (we say to ourselves "the narrator has no reason to lie about this"; or, "chances are he'll change his mind on that, just like he did before"; or, "this is unlikely to be true, given what the narrator said earlier about the same character"; or, "that could easily be wishful thinking"; or again, "how could he know what he's claiming here?"). Having done that, we also attach a *provisional assessment* ("that seems like good news, for now at least"; "this is presumably curtains, but let's wait and see"). And for each theory, we attach a *level of confidence* ("bunch of nonsense!"; or, "very deep!"; or, "didn't he say the opposite just two lines ago?").

Meanwhile, as new information comes in, we get in the habit of revising those values and those assessments. We get in the habit of rereading, reconsidering, thinking twice. The mistakes the novel virtually forces us to make—"too bad for me if the reader believes I take them for the truth"—do us a surprisingly important favor.

Why do mental habits like these matter, in the context of Proust? Well, remember what we saw in chapter 9: events in the future can reach back and transform the significance of events in the past. So we never know quite what will prove to have been significant, because what's coming next can radically change the meaning of things that are far behind us. (That makes it really helpful to store away as much information as possible.) And we also don't know, for any given episode, how it may end up contributing to the overall shape of our life; all we can do is make a provisional assessment or, in some cases, suspend judgment altogether.

Either way, we should probably re-evaluate from time to time, take stock, reconsider what we think we know. Our sense of the total picture is only ever partial and evolving; who knows, maybe someone we never paid attention to will turn out—"little did we know!"—to be the love of our life. Cognitive flexibility is going to stand us in very good stead.

So here's our sixth and most speculative explanation for why this is a novel—a formally intriguing novel, complete with unreliable narrator, intricate sentences, and mammoth scale—rather than a "traditional essay." Each of the novel's formal choices puts our

Three roads to yourself

If all of this is correct, then three of the six benefits on offer from Proust's novel are things that assist us in becoming who we are. First, the novel is an "optical instrument," revealing facets of our character that we didn't know, moving unconscious attitudes into the light of awareness. Second, it's a formal model, prompting us to imagine ways of thinking about our life as a story. And third, it's a mental gym, helping us retain and understand that story, revising and updating it as needs dictate. One of the most important things Proust's novel offers us is, perhaps, ourselves.

minds to work in a particular way, accumulating information, comparing comments, weighing probabilities, hypothesizing, testing, rereading, rethinking; that work serves as practice, strengthening the relevant neural pathways; and practice makes perfect (or at least, practice makes improved). We give a workout to our memory muscles, cultivate a habit of thinking twice, get better at storing things under advisement, strengthen our capacity for probabilistic reasoning. Reading this novel is going to the Proustian gym. If we're lucky, we'll end up with some powerful Proustian muscles.

Letting yourself be changed

I've listed six potential benefits from reading Proust's novel, and there may well be more besides. That could sound like way too many to be realistic, but then again, this novel is three thousand pages long. It took me seven years to read it. I wasn't deriving every benefit at every moment—the idea is only that we get all of them eventually, not all of them on each page—but my guess is that at least some of that seven-year stretch was spent learning about myself, some of it gaining insight into the world of an idiosyncratic author, some of it picking up skills I had no clue I was cultivating. A few of the benefits were definitely programmed in deliberately; others were *probably* intended; others still just came for free.

How many of those benefits turn on Proust's book being a novel, rather than a treatise? All but one. A treatise can easily inform us about the world—more efficiently, in fact, than a story can—but it has a harder time revealing my world, our world, or the world of the author, not to mention offering formal models for self-fashioning, let alone training grounds for the exercise of mental capacities. As Proust told Rivière, the *Search* has no choice but to include deliberate errors in order to do its phenomenological work.

And to serve as a Rorschach test, the *Search* also has to include deliberate *contradictions*. Swann, remember, falls in love with Odette for her availability and then, impossibly, falls in love with Odette (still for the first time!) for her unavailability. If you want to transmit some truths about the world, the most effective way to do so is to avoid contradictions like that, as well as errors like the end of *Swann's Way*; but if you want to recreate the feeling of an intellectual evolution, and reveal the reader to herself, they can be a brilliant move. Tempting the reader to make an interpretive decision and then holding up a mirror for her to see herself in? That's something only fiction can do.

As for the training, for that you need not just a novel but a *long* novel—maybe one that stretches over seven volumes, three thousand pages, 1.3 million words, months or years of our life. You need a novel because you need a kind of mental activity that is driven by literary form (unreliable narrator, intricate sentences): form fosters activity, activity constitutes practice, practice consolidates habits, and habits enhance a life. You need a long novel because the cultivation of habits takes time, iteration, persistence. Whatever we get from the *Search*, it comes not only from the extractable, detachable statements but, just as importantly, from the experience of reading, the months or years of effort and joy we spend in its company.

Isn't there something scandalous, though, about discussing the benefits of literature? Isn't art supposed to be valuable for its own sake? Don't we risk instrumentalizing great novels, reducing them to handy little self-help apps? ("Life hack: to know yourself better, read Proust.") It's true that there are inelegant ways of talking about what literature can do for us—but it seems strange to refrain altogether in the case of Proust, who himself was so forthright about them. Remember Proust saying, in 1913, that "the pleasure an artist gives us is that of discovering a whole new world"; remember his narrator issuing specific hopes for the

12. Having seen and admired some still life paintings, the narrator suddenly views the world around him in a new light.

impact of his future novel; and remember that same narrator spelling out, with some passion, the purpose and value of music, painting, and prose. After seeing a few of Elstir's still lifes, he is delighted to view after-dinner debris in a whole new light: "I would now happily remain at the table while it was being cleared.... I tried to find beauty there where I had never imagined before that it could exist, in the most ordinary things, in the profundities of 'still life' " (*BG*, 612-3). Neither he nor his creator appear to see anything wrong with allowing our aesthetic experiences to reach out loving tendrils and enlace other parts of our lives.

This artwork is designed, brilliantly, to affect us. We may as well let it.

A postscript for diehard Proust fans: Does the narrator write *In Search of Lost Time?*

At the end of *Time Regained*, the narrator gets inspired and finally starts writing a novel. The material for this novel, he tells us, will be "my past life" (*TR*, 304). So...surely he's writing *In Search of Lost Time?*

Well, maybe—but maybe not. That's definitely the majority view, but a few of us still hold out, Asterix-like, against the invaders. Why? Here are three reasons.

First, the narrator seems to know exactly what's in the book he's just written (which he usually calls his "story," or *récit*), but not what's in the book he's about to write (which he usually calls his "work," or *oeuvre*). That makes perfect sense if they're two separate texts, but not if they're the same.

Will his future novel portray a single face as having a "hundred different masks" (*TR*, 527) depending on who is looking at it and when? Will it depict passers-by as lacking nose, cheeks, and chin, since all we see when we glance their way is "a flickering reflection of our desires" (*TR*, 527)? He doesn't know: "if, in my attempt to transcribe a universe which had to be totally redrawn, I could not convey these changes and many others, the needfulness of which...has been made manifest in the course of my narrative [*ce récit*], at least I should not fail to portray man, in this universe, as endowed with the length not of his body but of his years" (*TR*, 528). If the two manuscripts are identical, then this sentence is truly bizarre. He knows perfectly well what's in the *récit*—that's what has "made manifest" the necessity to depict chinless strangers—so if the *oeuvre* is just the same thing, he should know what's in there too. He should really be clear, by now, as to whether the *oeuvre* "convey[s] these changes" or whether it doesn't. But somehow, he isn't.

Second, the book we've read frequently offers a preview of coming attractions (known in literary jargon as a "prolepsis"). After recounting an episode in *Swann's Way*, for example, the narrator promises us we'll learn more about its significance "in due course"—and we do, some 2,600 pages later. At the beginning of *Sodom and Gomorrah*, the narrator promises us we'll learn more about "a whole unconscious element of literary production"—and we do, some 2,000 pages further on.

That's not surprising in itself; the problem is that the person who embarks on a creative project in *Time Regained* is in mortal fear of dying at any moment (*TR*, 525). He's suffered a stroke, thinks of himself as an "old man" (*TR*, 350), and worries that he may well not live long enough to finish his book. (That's yet another important difference between Proust and his narrator: Proust had a hundred-page draft for his novel's conclusion by the age of thirty-seven (*MPG*, 113-240).) Are we supposed to think that this frail, anxious "old man" goes on to produce a work full of breezy prolepses, promising, with sublime confidence, material in volumes years away?

Last but not least, think about how obsessed the narrator is with Albertine, how passionate, how tormented, how devastated. And now compare that to what he tells us about his *oeuvre*: each female character, he says, will be "made up of numerous impressions derived from many girls" (*TR*, 510). (More generally, "beneath the name of every character of his invention [a novelist]

116

can put sixty names of characters that he has seen, one of whom has posed for the grimaces, another for the monocle, another for the fits of temper, another for the swaggering movement of his arm" (*TR*, 305).) As Leo Bersani has pointed out, this makes *The Captive* and *The Fugitive* very hard to understand, if they're supposed to be part of the narrator's future book. If Albertine were just the narrator's invention, based on a series of different people he knew, why would he tear his hair out trying to discover what's going on in her mind? Surely Albertine is *real* to him, a genuine individual, not a composite—unlike the female characters in the novel he's about to write.

So that's why some of us think the narrator's future novel is not *In Search of Lost Time*. But then again, many smart people have felt otherwise. Does the narrator end up writing the same book Proust did? You decide!

References

Preface

"Graphic novel": see Stéphane Heuet, *À la recherche du temps perdu, d'après l'oeuvre de Marcel Proust* (Paris: Guy Delcourt, 1998–2019).

"Modern technology": see Sara Danius, *The Senses of Modernism: Technology, Perception, and Aesthetics* (Ithaca, NY: Cornell University Press, 2002), 91–146; Suzanne Guerlac, *Proust, Photography, and the Time of Life: Ravaisson, Bergson, and Simmel* (London: Bloomsbury, 2020).

"Habit": see Samuel Beckett, *Proust/Three Dialogues* (London: Calder, 1965), 18–19; Gérard Genette, *Figures III* (Paris: Seuil, 1972), 111, 154.

"Symbolic geography": see Joshua Landy, *Philosophy as Fiction: Self, Deception, and Knowledge in Proust* (New York: Oxford University Press, 2004) (henceforth *PF*), 72–75.

"Metonymic metaphor": see Genette, *Figures III*, 41–63; Landy, *PF*, 68–75.

"The magic of names": see Roland Barthes, "Proust et les noms," in *Le degré zéro de l'écriture* (Paris: Seuil, 1972), 121–34.

"Complicated relationship to Henri Bergson": see Roger Shattuck, *Marcel Proust* (Princeton, NJ: Princeton University Press, 1982), 144–45; Georges Poulet, *Proustian Space*, trans. Elliott Coleman (Baltimore: Johns Hopkins University Press, 1977), 9–11; and Landy, *PF*, 7–8, 163.

"(Partial) love of discontinuity": see Poulet, *Proustian Space*, 37–40, 102.

119

Chapter 1: Art and life

"Some wonderful books": see in particular Jean-Yves Tadié, *Marcel Proust: A Life*, trans. Euan Cameron (New York: Penguin, 2000); William Carter, *Marcel Proust: A Life* (New Haven, CT: Yale University Press, 2000); and Adam Watt, *Marcel Proust* (London: Reaktion Books, 2013).

"The miracle of miracles": see Malcolm Bowie, "The Miracle of Miracles: Proust's Life and Losses, Before he Rose above Them," *TLS*, July 26, 2002, 4.

"Idolatry": see also Alain de Botton, *How Proust Can Change Your Life* (New York: Vintage, 1998), 193–96. For additional strengths and considerable weaknesses of *How Proust Can Change Your Life*, see Joshua Landy, *The World According to Proust* (New York: Oxford University Press, 2023) (henceforth *TWAP*), 116n6.

"Proust probably never ate a magic madeleine": see Landy, *PF*, 14–16. Contrast this with, for example, Robert Harrison's claim that "for Marcel Proust the taste of a madelaine [*sic*] brought to life a lost era of his childhood" (*Forests: The Shadow of Civilization* (Chicago: University of Chicago Press, 1992), 186).

"He had deleted the occasional stray 'Marcel'": see Michihiko Suzuki, "Le 'je' proustien," *Bulletin de la Société des amis de Marcel Proust* 9 (1959): 74. Jean-Yves Tadié adds (*Proust et le roman* (Paris: Gallimard, 1971), 24) that the longer Proust worked, the less autobiographical his novel became.

"The character isn't him": see Landy, *PF*, 14–24; Dorrit Cohn, "Proust's Generic Ambiguity," in *The Distinction of Fiction* (Baltimore: Johns Hopkins University Press, 1999), 58–78; Genette, *Figures III*, 256; and Gilles Deleuze, *Proust and Signs*, trans. Richard Howard (New York: George Braziller, 1972), 150.

"Gide reported Proust as saying": see André Gide, *Journal* (Paris: Gallimard, 1950), 694.

"An argument made by Elisabeth Ladenson": see Elisabeth Ladenson, *Proust's Lesbianism* (Ithaca, NY: Cornell University Press, 2007), 6, 7, 16, 50. The main proponent of the transposition theory was Justin O'Brien ("Albertine the Ambiguous: Notes on Proust's Transposition of Sexes," *PMLA* 64 (1949): 933–52). Its opponents include not just Ladenson but also Leo Bersani ("Death and Literary Authority," in *A New History of French Literature*, ed. Denis Hollier (Cambridge, MA: Harvard University Press, 1989), 865); Harry Levin (*The Gates of Horn: A Study of Five French*

Realists (Oxford: Oxford University Press, 1986), 414); and, to some extent, Edmund White (*Marcel Proust: A Life* (New York: Penguin, 1999), 24–25).

"It draws on a life, but its purpose isn't just to retell it": see Shattuck, *Marcel Proust*, 20, 150–51.

Chapter 2: Plot and character

"In this otherwise gloomy period": see Landy, *PF*, 216-17n27, for why it may make sense to place the madeleine at that point in the chronology. For a different theory, see Gareth Steel, *Chronology and Time in "À la Recherche du temps perdu"* (Geneva: Droz, 1979), 58.

"A meeting of minds": cf. Shattuck, *Marcel Proust*, 160.

"Imprinted with their subjectivity": cf. Leo Bersani, *Marcel Proust: The Fictions of Life and of Art* (Oxford: Oxford University Press, 1965), 154.

"High society, travel, and friendship haven't done much": compare to some extent Deleuze, who talks of the various "worlds" the narrator moves through (society, friendship, love, nature) before reaching that of art.

"Self and world meet": see Bersani, *Marcel Proust*, esp. 186. In the seminar we taught together at Chicago, Robert Pippin spoke movingly and memorably about feeling at home in the world. I owe him a huge debt of gratitude for that class, those lunches, and all the ideas they inspired.

"Wine and wafer": see Landy, *PF*, 182n101.

Chapter 3: Memories and impressions

"Proust wasn't the first": see Richard Terdiman, *Present Past: Modernity and the Memory Crisis* (Ithaca, NY: Cornell University Press, 1993), 187–98.

"You also remember being you": see Landy, *PF*, 110–13.

"Isn't this really just 'nostalgia'?": see Landy, *PF*, 215-16n22.

"Not necessarily the content": see Genette, *Figures III*, 95.

"Some critics have wondered how plausible this is": for example Terdiman, *Present Past*, 185, 237.

"Some readers of Proust have run impressions together with involuntary memories": one example is Deleuze, *Proust and Signs*, 12. Bersani, by contrast, carefully marks the distinction (*Marcel Proust*, 225–28).

"The steeples at Martinville": see Landy, *PF*, 51–84.

"Sometimes they're idiosyncratic": cf. Bersani, *Marcel Proust*, 207; see also Ernst Robert Curtius, *Marcel Proust* (Frankfurt: Suhrkamp Verlag, 1961), chapters 25 and 26.

"The professional cynics out there": these professional cynics include Vincent Descombes, *Proust: Philosophy of the Novel*, trans. Catherine Chance Macksey (Stanford, CA: Stanford University Press, 1992), 154–55, 214–17, 268–69.

Chapter 4: Love and sex

"Brilliant essay": see Hervé Picherit, "The Impossibly Many Loves of Charles Swann: The Myth of Proustian Love and the Reader's 'Impression' in *Un amour de Swann*," *Poetics Today* 28, no. 4 (2007): 619–52.

"Run and hide": many books about Proust simply accept the pessimistic picture at face value. In Proust, such books claim, love always involves jealousy (Richard Bales, *Proust: "À la recherche du temps perdu"* (London: Grant & Cutler, 1995), 56); is never reciprocated (Bersani, *Marcel Proust*, 185); and/or always makes us miserable (Justin O'Brien, *The Maxims of Marcel Proust* (New York: Columbia, 1948), 110–11).

"Doesn't entirely hold up": cf. Landy, *PF*, 26–28.

"Gabrielle Elstir": cf. Landy, *PF*, 27.

"Mme de Villeparisis": cf. Morris Weitz, *Philosophy in Literature: Shakespeare, Voltaire, Tolstoy and Proust* (Detroit: Wayne State University Press, 1963), 84.

"Only apply to him": see Bersani, *Marcel Proust*, 237–38.

"Some people would never have fallen in love": see François duc de La Rochefoucauld, *Maxims*, trans. Leonard Tancock (London: Penguin, 1959), maxim #136.

"Why his theories on the subject are so spectacularly incoherent": cf. Eve Kosofsky Sedgwick, *Epistemology of the Closet* (Berkeley: University of California Press, 2008), 217–20; Ladenson, *Proust's Lesbianism*, 41n29; Erin Carlston, *Double Agents* (New York: Columbia University Press, 2013), 7, 99; and Landy, *PF*, 34.

Ulrichs: see Ladenson, *Proust's Lesbianism*, 12, 39.

"Shift in orientation": for evidence that this really is a shift, see Landy, *TWAP*, 118n26.

"Doesn't even try to explain": see Ladenson, *Proust's Lesbianism*, 50.

"Erin Carlston's analysis": see Carlston, *Double Agents*, especially 114–15, 121, 137–39.

"He periodically changes his mind": Malcolm Bowie makes this point
    in *Freud, Proust, and Lacan: Theory as Fiction* (Cambridge:
    Cambridge University Press, 1987), 47.

"Proust told critic Jacques Rivière": see Marcel Proust,
    Correspondance, vol. 13 (Paris: Plon, 1985), 98–100.

"Important not to go to the other extreme": for examples of scholars
    who appear to have done just that, see Joshua Landy, "Why Proust
    Isn't an 'Essayist,' and Why It Matters," *Romanic Review* 111, no. 3
    (2020): 392–407.

"It makes him feel better about things": on this point, see Duncan
    Large, *Nietzsche and Proust: A Comparative Study* (Oxford:
    Oxford University Press, 2001), 138.

Chapter 5: Knowledge and ignorance

"This perspective prevents us": cf. Landy, *PF*, 51–84.

"Above all, it endows them with a value": cf. Alexander Nehamas, *The
    Art of Living: Socratic Reflections from Plato to Foucault*
    (Berkeley: University of California Press, 1998), 148.

"Split the difference": cf. Bowie, *Freud, Proust and Lacan*, 54.

"Some interpreters": see Rick Furtak, "Love, Subjectivity, and Truth in
    Proust," *Partial Answers: Journal of Literature and the History of
    Ideas* 21, no. 1 (2023): 53–70; Martha Nussbaum, *Love's
    Knowledge: Essays on Philosophy and Literature* (Oxford: Oxford
    University Press, 1990), 271. Cf. also Descombes, *Proust*, 42;
    Richard Terdiman, *The Dialectics of Isolation: Self and Society in
    the French Novel from the Realists to Proust* (New Haven, CT: Yale
    University Press, 1976), 201.

"Sometimes illusions are far more valuable": see Landy, *PF*, 85–100;
    Rosemary Lloyd, *Closer and Closer Apart: Jealousy in Literature*
    (Ithaca, NY: Cornell University Press, 1995), 61; Bowie, *Freud,
    Proust and Lacan*, 58.

"Midway through volume 2": Walter Benjamin calls this the "decisive
    passage in Proust concerning the aura." Walter Benjamin, *The
    Arcades Project*, trans. Howard Eiland and Kevin McLaughlin
    (Cambridge, MA: Harvard University Press, 1999), 560.

Chapter 6: Inclusion and exclusion

"A wonderful chapter by Edward Hughes": see Edward J. Hughes,
    "Proust and Social Spaces," in *The Cambridge Companion to*

Proust, ed. Richard Bales (Cambridge: Cambridge University Press, 2001), 151–67, 172, 176.

"To paraphrase Hughes again": see Hughes, "Proust and Social Spaces," 154. See also Bersani, *Marcel Proust*, 172.

"The decline of the aristocracy": see Hughes, "Proust and Social Spaces," 165; Bersani, *Marcel Proust*, 176; Cynthia Gamble, "From Belle Epoque to First World War: The Social Panorama," in *The Cambridge Companion to Proust*, ed. Richard Bales (Cambridge: Cambridge University Press, 2001), 9.

"Perhaps symbolically": see Brigitte Mahuzier, "The First World War," in *Marcel Proust in Context*, ed. Adam Watt (Cambridge: Cambridge University Press, 2013), 179.

Chapter 7: Art and artists

"Art isn't just a better community": for various benefits of literature, see Joshua Landy, *How to Do Things with Fictions* (New York: Oxford University Press, 2012), 4–8.

"A hybrid": for "hybrids," see Landy, *PF*, 11.

"We need a detour": see Landy, *PF*, 80, 144, 198n60.

"My business is to draw what I see": John Ruskin reported this anecdote in *The Eagle's Nest: Ten Lectures on the Relation of Natural Science to Art, Given before the University of Oxford in Lent Term, 1872* (New York: John Wiley & Sons, 1880), 111.

"That's the miracle of literature": see Simone de Beauvoir, *Que peut la littérature?* (Paris: Union générale d'éditions, 1965), 82.

"Reading cannot be sustained": see Jacques Normand (under the pen name Jacques Madeleine), "En somme, qu'est-ce?," in *Les critiques de notre temps et Proust*, ed. Jacques Bersani (Paris: Garnier, 1971), 13–20.

"Everything constantly grew from the middle": cf. Terdiman, *Dialectics of Isolation*, 181. On the evolution of Proust's novel more generally, see Alison Finch, *Proust's Additions: The Making of "A la recherche du temps perdu"* (Cambridge: Cambridge University Press, 1977); Marion Schmid, "The Birth and Development of *À la recherche du temps perdu*," in *The Cambridge Companion to Proust*, ed. Richard Bales (Cambridge: Cambridge University Press, 2001), 58–73.

"Seneca put it nicely": see Seneca, *Letters from a Stoic: Epistulae Morales ad Lucilium*, trans. Robin Campbell (London: Penguin, 2004), letter 28.

"Where he finds enchantment is here on earth": cf. Joshua Landy and
Michael Saler, "The Varieties of Modern Enchantment," in *The
Re-Enchantment of the World: Secular Magic in a Rational Age*,
ed. Joshua Landy and Michael Saler (Stanford, CA: Stanford
University Press, 2009), 1–14.

"The world has become 'infinite' for us all over again": see Friedrich
Nietzsche, *The Gay Science*, trans. Walter Kaufmann (New York:
Random House, 1974), section 374.

"A huge favor": see Shattuck, *Marcel Proust*, 164–65; Joshua Landy,
"'Un égoïsme utilisable pour autrui': Le statut normatif de
l'auto-description chez Proust," in *Morales de Proust*, ed. Mariolina
Bertini and Antoine Compagnon (Paris: L'Harmattan,
2010), 83–99.

"Borrowing the structure of the septet": see Landy, *PF*, 139–40.

"A single cadence": the notion of "cadence" is drawn from J. David
Velleman, "Narrative Explanation," *Philosophical Review* 112, no. 1
(2003): 6.

Chapter 8: Intellect and intuition

"Proust never read a word of Freud": see Tadié, *Marcel Proust*, 480.

"While reading myself": see Marcel Proust, *Correspondance*, vol. 12
(Paris: Plon, 1984), 180.

"Large numbers of intellectuals": see Henri F. Ellenberger, *The
Discovery of the Unconscious: The History and Evolution of
Dynamic Psychiatry* (New York: Basic Books, 1970).

"An alternative possibility": see Georges Poulet, *Studies in Human
Time*, trans. Elliott Coleman (Baltimore: Johns Hopkins University
Press, 1956), 296. See also Deleuze, *Proust and Signs*, 86–87.

Chapter 9: True self and total self

"Any sense of stable identity": for this question and chapter 9 as a
whole, cf. Landy, *PF*, 101–27.

"Added urgency": see Robert B. Pippin, *Henry James and Modern
Moral Life* (Cambridge: Cambridge University Press, 2001),
chapter 1; Charles Taylor, *Sources of the Self: The Making of the
Modern Identity* (Cambridge: Cambridge University Press, 1989),
28; Bernard Williams, *Truth and Truthfulness: An Essay in
Genealogy* (Princeton, NJ: Princeton University Press, 2004), 301;

and Lionel Trilling, *Sincerity and Authenticity* (Cambridge, MA: Harvard University Press, 1972), 19, 24.

"I am large, I contain multitudes": see Walt Whitman, "Song of Myself," in *Leaves of Grass* (Minneapolis: University of Minnesota Press, 1966), 55.

"One or two decent arguments in the other direction": I list more of these arguments in Joshua Landy, "Lyric Self-Fashioning: Shakespeare's 'Sonnet 35' as Formal Model," *Philosophy and Literature* 45, no. 1 (2021): 236–38 and Joshua Landy, "Saving the Self from Stories: Resistance to Narrative in Primo Levi's *Periodic Table*," *Narrative* 30, no. 1 (2022): 98–99n38.

"There's also the issue of decision-making": here I'm drawing on Christine Korsgaard, "Personal Identity and the Unity of Agency: A Kantian Response to Parfit," *Philosophy and Public Affairs* 18, no. 2 (1989): 110.

"Like Hamlet": see Joshua Landy, "To Thine Own Selves Be True-ish: Shakespeare's *Hamlet* as Formal Model," in *Shakespeare's "Hamlet": Philosophical Perspectives*, ed. Tzachi Zamir (New York: Oxford University Press, 2018), 154–87.

"Excited to see how things turn out": see Luca Ferrero, "What Good Is a Diachronic Will?," *Philosophical Studies* 144 (2009): 403–30.

"See our setbacks and challenges in a whole new light": see R. Lanier Anderson, "Nietzsche on Truth, Illusion, and Redemption," *European Journal of Philosophy* 13, no. 2 (2005): 185–225. Anderson is building on the work of Alexander Nehamas in *Nietzsche: Life as Literature* (Cambridge, MA: Harvard University Press, 1985); Nehamas in turn is building on Nietzsche, including parts of *Zarathustra* and sections 78, 107, 290, 299, and 341 of *The Gay Science*.

"In a concert of instruments": see Michel de Montaigne, *The Complete Essays of Montaigne*, trans. Donald Frame (Stanford, CA: Stanford University Press, 1952), 711.

"If you can picture your life as a story...it starts to hang together": see Nehamas, *Nietzsche*, chapter 5. Nehamas makes the connection to Proust on 167–69, 188.

"Two ways of recounting a series of events": see Boris Tomashevsky, "Thematics," in *Russian Formalist Criticism: Four Essays*, ed. Lee T. Lemon and Marion J. Reis, trans. Lee T. Lemon and Marion J. Reis (Lincoln: University of Nebraska Press, 1965), 66; Suzanne Keen, *Narrative Form* (London: Palgrave, 2004), 74.

"Antoine Compagnon": see especially his series of lectures, "Morales de
    Proust," available at https://www.college-de-france.fr/fr/agenda/
    cours/morales-de-proust.

"A point Robert Pippin makes": see Robert Pippin, "On 'Becoming
    Who One Is' (and Failing): Proust's Problematic Selves," in *The
    Persistence of Subjectivity: On the Kantian Aftermath* (Cambridge:
    Cambridge University Press, 2005), 307–38.

"Getting known": see Samuel Beckett, *Collected Shorter Plays* (New
    York: Grove Press, 1984), 62.

"One cannot become a great writer all by oneself": see Descombes,
    Proust, 280.

"Your story can only ever be provisional": see Landy, *PF*, 120–22;
    Pippin, "On 'Becoming Who One Is,'" 309.

"Exchange in *Don Quixote*": see Miguel de Cervantes Saavedra, *The
    Adventures of Don Quixote*, trans. J. M. Cohen (Baltimore:
    Penguin, 1970), 177.

"Reaches back and changes the past": cf. J. David Velleman,
    "Well-Being and Time," in *The Metaphysics of Death*, ed. John
    Martin Fischer (Stanford, CA: Stanford University Press, 1993),
    339–40.

"How amazing the structure is": see also J. P. Houston, "Temporal
    Patterns in *À la recherche du temps perdu*," *French Studies* 16, no. 1
    (1962): 33–44; Genette, *Figures III*, 141–42; and Jean Rousset,
    *Forme et signification: Essai sur les structures littéraires de
    Corneille à Claudel* (Paris: José Corti, 1995), 138–45.

Chapter 10: Why a novel?

"What's so special about fiction?": for this whole chapter, see Joshua
    Landy, "Why a Novel?," in *Marcel Proust's "In Search of Lost Time":
    Philosophical Perspectives*, ed. Katherine Elkins (New York:
    Oxford University Press, 2022), 19–46. I am grateful to Oxford for
    letting me reuse some of the material here.

"The story of a morning": letter to Anna de Noailles from mid-
    December 1908, in Proust, *Correspondance*, vol. 8 (Paris: Plon,
    1981), 320–21.

"An ingenious answer": see Picherit, "Impossibly Many Loves," 642–50.

"The novel is full of beautiful moments like this": see Gaëtan Picon,
    Lecture de Proust (Paris: Gallimard, 1995), 64.

"No life after death": cf. Shattuck, *Marcel Proust*, 145–46.

"The phenomenology of human experience": on fiction and phenomenology, cf. Milan Kundera, *The Art of the Novel*, trans. Linda Asher (New York: Harper, 1986), 32.

"Simulates the experience of involuntary memory": see Joseph Frank, "Spatial Form in Modern Literature," in *The Widening Gyre* (New Brunswick, NJ: Rutgers University Press, 1963), 20, 23. E. M. Forster also says something a little bit like this in *Aspects of the Novel* (London: Edward Arnold, 1974), 114.

"Highly organized machines": see Landy, *PF*, 129–45; Jean Milly, *La phrase de Proust: Des phrases de Bergotte aux phrases de Vinteuil* (Paris: Larousse, 1975), 164–87; and Leo Spitzer, "Le style de Marcel Proust," in *Études de style*, trans. Éliane Kaufholz, Alain Coulon, and Michel Foucault (Paris: Gallimard, 1970), 400–402.

"A training-ground for our mind": see Landy, *PF*, 143–45; see also Darci L. Gardner, "Rereading as a Mechanism of Defamiliarization in Proust," *Poetics Today* 37, no. 1 (2016): 55–105. Descombes seems at one point to say something similar (35), but most of the time he presents Proust's novel as "a demonstration" (299), its point being to tell us things (241), show things (246), establish things (299), offer commentary on things (133), and teach lessons on things (193).

"We attach a probabilistic value": these sentences were inspired by a very helpful conversation I had with Ting Zheng, to whom I'm most grateful.

"We get in the habit of rereading": cf. Milly, *La phrase de Proust*, 202.

"Others still just came for free": cf. Descombes, *Proust*, 6, 233.

A postscript for diehard Proust fans: Does the narrator write *In Search of Lost Time*?

"A few of us still hold out": members of the Gaulish village include Landy, *PF*, 36–47; Antoine Compagnon, *Proust entre deux siècles* (Paris: Seuil, 1989), 301–2; Nicola Luckhurst, *Science and Structure in Proust's "À la recherche du temps perdu"* (Oxford: Oxford University Press, 2000), 8; Marcel Muller, *Les voix narratives dans la "Recherche du temps perdu"* (Geneva: Droz, 1965), 49; Roland Barthes, "Longtemps, je me suis couché de bonne heure," in *The Rustle of Language*, trans. Richard Howard (New York: Hill & Wang, 1986), 283; and Pierre-Louis Rey and Brian Rogers, "Notice," in Proust, *À la recherche du temps perdu* (Paris: Gallimard, 1988), 1174–75.

"That's yet another important difference": cf. Shattuck, *Marcel Proust*, 151.

"As Leo Bersani has pointed out": see Bersani, *Marcel Proust*, 195. Bersani draws a different conclusion, since he believes "the novel we are reading is a novel written by [the narrator]" (195). For discussion, see Landy, *TWAP*, 129n7.

"Many smart people have felt otherwise": the best argument I've read to date is Jonas Aaron-Hertel's "Does Marcel Finish His Novel?" (unpublished manuscript). But see also Bersani, *Marcel Proust*, 244; Nehamas, *Nietzsche*, 168.

Further reading

Beckett, Samuel. *Proust / Three Dialogues*. London: Calder, 1965.

Bersani, Leo. *Marcel Proust: The Fictions of Life and of Art*. Oxford: Oxford University Press, 1965.

Benhaïm, André. *Panim: Visages de Proust*. Paris: Presses Universitaires du Septentrion, 2006.

Bouillaguet, Annick, and Brian G. Rogers. *Dictionnaire Marcel Proust*. Paris: Honoré Champion, 2005.

Bowie, Malcolm. *Freud, Proust and Lacan: Theory as Fiction*. Cambridge: Cambridge University Press, 1987.

Bowie, Malcolm. *Proust among the Stars*. London: Harper Collins, 1998.

Carlston, Erin. *Double Agents*. New York: Columbia University Press, 2013.

Carter, William. *Marcel Proust: A Life*. New Haven, CT: Yale University Press, 2000.

Compagnon, Antoine. *Proust entre deux siècles*. Paris: Seuil, 1989.

Curtius, Ernst Robert. *Marcel Proust*. Frankfurt: Suhrkamp Verlag, 1961.

Deleuze, Gilles. *Proust and Signs*. Translated by Richard Howard. New York: George Braziller, 1972.

Descombes, Vincent. *Proust: Philosophy of the Novel*. Translated by Catherine Chance Macksey. Stanford, CA: Stanford University Press, 1992.

Fraisse, Luc. *L'éclectisme philosophique de Marcel Proust*. Paris: Presses de l'Université Paris-Sorbonne, 2013.

Genette, Gérard. *Figures III*. Paris: Seuil, 1972. Largely translated by
    Jane E. Lewin as *Narrative Discourse: An Essay in Method*. Ithaca,
    NY: Cornell University Press, 1980.

Guerlac, Suzanne. *Proust, Photography, and the Time of Life:
    Ravaisson, Bergson, and Simmel*. London: Bloomsbury, 2020.

Hughes, Edward J. *Proust, Class, and Nation*. Oxford: Oxford
    University Press, 2011.

Ladenson, Elisabeth. *Proust's Lesbianism*. Ithaca, NY: Cornell
    University Press, 2007.

Landy, Joshua. *Philosophy as Fiction: Self, Deception, and Knowledge
    in Proust*. New York: Oxford University Press, 2004.

Large, Duncan. *Nietzsche and Proust: A Comparative Study*. Oxford:
    Oxford University Press, 2001.

Lucey, Michael. *What Proust Heard: Novels and the Ethnography of
    Talk*. Chicago: University of Chicago Press, 2022.

Luckhurst, Nicola. *Science and Structure in Proust's "À la recherche du
    temps perdu."* Oxford: Oxford University Press, 2000.

McDonald, Christie, and François Proulx, eds. *Proust and the Arts*.
    Cambridge: Cambridge University Press, 2015.

Milly, Jean. *La phrase de Proust: Des phrases de Bergotte aux phrases
    de Vinteuil*. Paris: Larousse, 1975.

Muller, Marcel. *Les voix narratives dans la "Recherche du temps
    perdu."* Geneva: Droz, 1965.

Picon, Gaëtan. *Lecture de Proust*. Paris: Gallimard, 1995.

Poulet, Georges. *Proustian Space*. Translated by Elliott Coleman.
    Baltimore: Johns Hopkins University Press, 1977.

Rogers, Brian. *Proust's Narrative Techniques*. Geneva: Droz, 1965.

Sedgwick, Eve Kosofsky. *Epistemology of the Closet*. Berkeley:
    University of California Press, 2008.

Shattuck, Roger. *Marcel Proust*. Princeton, NJ: Princeton University
    Press, 1982.

Simon, Anne. *Proust ou le réel retrouvé: Le sensible et son expression
    dans "À la recherche du temps perdu."* Paris: Honoré
    Champion, 2011.

Steel, Gareth. *Chronology and Time in "À la Recherche du temps
    perdu."* Geneva: Droz, 1979.

Tadié, Jean-Yves. *Proust et le roman*. Paris: Gallimard, 1971.

Tadié, Jean-Yves. *Marcel Proust: A Life*. Translated by Euan Cameron.
    New York: Penguin, 2000.

Terdiman, Richard. *The Dialectics of Isolation: Self and Society in the French Novel from the Realists to Proust*. New Haven, CT: Yale University Press, 1976.

Watt, Adam. *The Cambridge Introduction to Marcel Proust*. Cambridge, UK: Cambridge University Press, 2011.

Index

For the benefit of digital users, indexed terms that span two pages (e.g., 52–53) may, on occasion, appear on only one of those pages.

A

Albertine Simonet (fictional character, primary love interest of narrator) 7, 9–10, 12, 15, 24–5, 27, 30–1, 33–7, 44–6, 48, 50, 74–7, 79, 95–6, 98, 105, 110, 116–17
Albertine's mole 40, 44, 104
Andrée (fictional character, potential love interest of narrator) 30
antisemitism 56–8
art
  as catalyst 39
  ethics of 73–4
  as expression of artist's vision ("her world") 14, 64–74, 101–3, 106, 108, 112
  as formal model 74–6, 101–2, 106–8, 111–12
  impact on love 76
  as means of enchantment 13–15, 69–73, 81
  not connected to the artist's biography xxv, 1–3

  as Rorschach test ("my world") 63, 74, 101–3, 106, 108, 111–13
  as route to genuine connection 13, 66–72
  as route to knowledge ("the world") 38–9, 62–3, 74, 109
  as stock of phenomenological data ("our world") 42–3, 64, 74, 101–4, 106, 108–9, 112
  as training ground 108–13
  as transfiguration 73–4
autobiography (Proust's novel not being one) 3–8, 17, 39

B

Beauvoir, Simone de 68
Beckett, Samuel xxiii–xxiv, 97
Bergotte (fictional character, novelist) 2, 10, 27, 60, 62–3, 65–6, 96
Bergson, Henri xxv, 79, 81–2
Bersani, Leo 116–17
Bible of Amiens, The (Ruskin) 4
bisexuality 7, 34, 37, 48
Bowie, Malcolm 2–3

C

Captive, The (Proust) 107, 116–17
Carlston, Erin 37
Cervantes, Miguel de 97
Charcot, Jean-Martin 79
Charlus, Baron Palamède de (most prominent gay character in the novel, aristocrat, brilliant aesthete) 26–7, 29–30, 33–7, 44, 48, 55, 60–1, 78–9, 95–6
Christianity 15–16, 56–8, 60–1, 72
chronicle *vs.* narrative 94
cognitive flexibility 108–12
coherence of character 84–5
collective identity 56
communities
    of aesthetic appreciation 60–1
    class-based 55–62
    national 37–8
    of sexual orientation 37–8
Compagnon, Antoine 95–6
Cottard (fictional character, doctor) 2, 55–6
Crécy, Odette de. *See* Odette de Crécy

D

Descombes, Vincent 97
Double Agents (Carlston) 37
Dreyfus, Alfred 37
Dreyfus affair 37, 56–8, 60–1
Duchesse de Guermantes. *See* Guermantes, Duchesse de

E

egoism 46, 73–4
Elstir (fictional character, painter, happily married) 2, 10, 15, 29–31, 33, 38, 55, 59–60, 62, 64–7, 70, 96, 103–4, 107
enchantment 15. *See also* art
ethics of art 73–4
Eulenburg, Philipp von 56–7

everyday language *vs.* literary language 67
exclusion. *See* inclusion

F

feeling of remembering 105–6
Françoise (fictional character, housekeeper) xxv, 56–7
Freud, Sigmund 78–80
Fugitive, The (Proust) 116–17

G

Gide, André 1, 7, 33–4
Gilberte Swann. *See* Swann, Gilberte
Goncourt prize 1
great cup of tea 102
Guermantes, Duchesse de (fictional character, aristocrat, love interest of sorts for narrator) 6–7, 9–10, 27, 30, 32, 37, 46, 49–50, 55, 95–6
Guermantes, Princesse de (fictional character, aristocrat) 55

H

habit
    bad kind 13–14
    good kind 110–12
heterosexuality 33–4, 56–7
high society 55–62
"hommes-femmes" theory 37
homosexuality. *See* same-sex desire

I

identity
    collective 56
    national 37–8
    social 97
identity, personal. *See also* self
    difficulty of achieving 87–90

importance of 83–7
search for 12–14, 62
"idolatry" (aesthetic) 3–4, 73
Illiers, France (a town which is not
  Combray) 2–5, 17, 73
illusion 51–3, 65
  lucid 51, 54
  necessary 53–4
  valuable 51–3
"impressions" *vs.* memories 21–2, 62
inclusion and exclusion 56–8
inner life (importance of) 24–5
In Search of Lost Time (Proust)
  an attempt at summarizing 9–14
  as conduit to Proust's vision 103–4
  as formal model 106–8
  as "optical instrument," 102–3
  as stock of phenomenological
    data 103–4
  as training ground 108–13
  its benefits to reader 108–14
  its impact on twentieth-century
    fiction xxv, 1–2
  its plot as the story of a
    vocation 12–15, 95, 107
  not an autobiography 6, 8, 39
  not a treatise 29–30, 38–41,
    104, 109–10
  not the narrator's future
    novel 12, 115–17
  producing the feeling of
    remembering 105–6
  really a search for purpose,
    identity, belonging,
    connection, and enchantment
    xxv, 12–16, 42, 62, 72, 85, 92, 95
insiders and outsiders 56–60
instinct 49, 80–1
intellect and intuition 28, 42,
    44–5, 48–50, 88, 92–3
  clashing in jealousy 48–50
  clashing in knowledge of
    others 48–50, 80–1
  clashing in knowledge of the
    world 44–5, 80–1, 104

combined in aesthetic
    creation 81, 92–3
combined in involuntary
    memory 81–2, 92–3, 105–6
combined in knowledge of
    oneself 81, 92–3
combined in lucid illusion
    81, 92–3
as conscious and unconscious
    mind 80–2
intuition. *See also* intellect and
    intuition
  a torment machine 49
involuntary memory 4–6, 12,
    17–22, 81–2, 105–6
  as evidence for true self 19–22,
    62, 90–1, 99
  vs. nostalgia 19–21
  yielding both past self and true
    self 19, 62, 90–1

J

jealousy 9–10, 28–31, 44, 49–50,
    81, 92–3
Jewishness 6, 37, 56–8, 60–1

K

knowledge. *See also* intellect and
    intuition
  by acquaintance 47–8
  of facts 44–5, 47
  of others 47–50, 56, 80–1
  of self (*see* self-knowledge)
  through art 39, 62–3, 74, 109
  of truths 45, 47, 53
  of what not to know 50–4
Krafft-Ebing, Richard von 35–6

L

Ladenson, Elisabeth 7, 37
learning from fiction ("dangerous")
    39, 109

lesbianism. *See* same-sex desire
level of confidence (in reading) 110
literary *vs.* everyday language 68
love
    first moment(s) of 26, 32–3,
        102–3, 113
    imitation and 33, 41
    jealousy and (*see* jealousy)
    narrator's depressing theory
        of 38–41
    officially illusory and
        destructive 28
    officially based on projection 27
    officially interchangeable 26–8
    product of our temperament
        31–2, 91
    revelatory of true self 47
    same-sex 6–7, 26–7, 33–8, 41,
        44, 59–60
    sometimes enduring 29–31
    sometimes happy 29
    sometimes produced by anxiety
        32, 102
    sometimes produced by art
        32, 76, 102
    sometimes produced by good
        tea 102
    sometimes produced by hope
        30, 32, 102

M

madeleine episode xxiii, 4–6, 12
Martinville steeples 21–3, 42–3,
    46–7, 51, 90–1, 99
memory
    feeling of 105–6
    "impressions" and 21–2
    involuntary (*see* involuntary
        memory)
    voluntary 18–19
Montaigne, Michel de 93
morality and immorality 33,
    55–6, 95–6

Moreau, Gustave 40, 66
Morel, Bénédict 35–6
Morel, Charlie (fictional character,
    partner of Charlus) 26–7,
    34, 95–6

N

narrative *vs.* chronicle 94
narrator, the (main character of
    Proust's novel)
    not identical to Proust
        5–8, 38–41
    sometimes right about things
        xxv–xxvi, 40–1
national identity 37–8
necessary illusions 45, 54
Nietzsche, Friedrich 72, 79
Noailles, Anna de 101
Normand, Jacques 69
Norpois, Baron de (fictional
    character, diplomat)
    29–30
no-self theory, the 85
nostalgia *vs.* involuntary
    memory 19–21

O

objective reality 43–5
Odette de Crécy (fictional character,
    love interest of Swann) 26,
    30–4, 37, 48, 64–5, 70, 80,
    88–9, 102–3, 113
optical illusions 65
outsiders. *See* insiders

P

perspective
    universal aspect 42–3
    individual aspect 22–5, 42–3,
        65, 90–1
Picherit, Hervé 26, 32, 102

Pippin, Robert 96
Poulet, Georges 80
Princesse de Guermantes.
　　See Guermantes, Princesse de
Proust's Lesbianism (Ladenson) 7

R

Rachel (fictional character,
　　talented actress, Robert's
　　surprising girlfriend)
　　34–5, 88–9
Rivière, Jacques 38–9, 104,
　　109, 112
Robert de Saint-Loup. *See*
　　Saint-Loup, Robert de
Ruskin, John xxv–xxvi, 4, 39
Russian Revolution 59

S

Sainte-Beuve, Charles
　　Augustin 1–2, 66
Saint-Loup, Robert de (fictional
　　character, aristocrat,
　　narrator's best friend) 9–10,
　　12, 29–30, 34–5, 37, 44, 55,
　　88–9, 95–6
same-sex desire xxv, 6–7, 33–8, 41,
　　44, 59–60
　　female 7, 26–7, 48
　　male 6–7, 33–8, 48, 60–1
　　and problem of other minds 48
　　and semi-ideal community
　　　37–8
Schopenhauer, Arthur 79
self-deception 81, 92–3
self, everyday *vs.* creative 2–3, 5,
　　66, 90–1
self-fashioning 62, 96–7, 101–2, 112
self-knowledge 45–7, 50–1,
　　63, 81, 95
　　by reading good novels 63,
　　　91, 102–3

by working back from behavior
　　46–7, 91
by working back from creation
　　66–8
by working back from
　　projection 23–4
self, problems with
　　conformity 56, 74, 83, 88
　　division into aspects 88
　　fragmentation in a moment
　　　xxv, 83–90
　　inconsistency across time
　　　xxv, 83–90
　　rejection by some thinkers 85
self, solutions for
　　endurance of true self 5, 90–2
　　"harmony" in a moment
　　　92–3
　　uniqueness of true self 21–4, 33,
　　　43, 64–5, 83, 91
　　wholeness across time
　　　xxv, 94–100
shape of a life 106–8
Simonet, Albertine.
　　See Albertine Simonet
social mobility 58–9
Sodom and Gomorrah
　　(Proust) 34, 116
Stermaria, Alix de (fictional
　　character, brief love interest of
　　narrator) 7
style 14, 68–70, 91
　　of Proust's novel xxv, 91–2,
　　　101–14
subjective idealism 44
summarizing *In Search of Lost
　　Time* 7, 9–14
surprise and objective reality
　　43–5
Swann, Charles (fictional character,
　　Jewish member of high society,
　　family friend) 3–4, 7, 9–10, 12,
　　26, 29–34, 37, 55, 58, 60–1, 70,
　　80–1, 102, 113

Index

Swann, Gilberte (fictional character, daughter of Charles and Odette, adolescent love interest of narrator) 7, 9–10, 27, 30–1, 37, 39, 53–4, 76–7, 98, 105
Swann's Way (Proust) 1, 69, 99, 113, 116

T

Tamassia, Arrigo 35–6
Tarde, Gabriel 33, 35
Time Regained (Proust) 58, 62, 93, 107, 115–16
train travel *vs.* car travel 51–3
truth. *See* knowledge
Turner, J. M. W. 64

U

Ulrichs, Karl Heinrich 35–6
unconscious (non-Freudian) 45–6, 78–80
unity. *See* self, solutions for

V

Verdurin, M and Mme (fictional characters, underwhelming salon hosts) 55–7, 60, 95–6
Vinteuil, Mlle (fictional character, daughter of Vinteuil) 44, 60–1, 95–6
Vinteuil (fictional character, composer) 2, 6, 10, 15, 32, 34, 60–2, 65–6, 70, 74–5, 88, 96, 102, 106, 108
vision. *See* art
voluntary memory 18–19

W

wasted time 55–8
Whitman, Walt 84–5
wholeness. *See* self, solutions for
Wilde, Oscar 7, 34, 56–7